Congress and Democracy

Congress and Democracy

David J. Vogler
Wheaton College

Sidney R. Waldman
Haverford College

A division of Congressional Quarterly Inc.
1414 22nd Street N.W., Washington, D.C. 20037

Printed in the United States of America

Library of Congress Cataloging in Publication Data

Vogler, David J.
   Congress and Democracy.

   Includes index.
   1. United States.   Congress.   2. Representative
government and representation—United States.
3. Democracy.   I. Waldman, Sidney R.,   1940-
II. Title.
JK1061.V6   1985   328.73   85-12801
ISBN 0-87187-378-8

To Andrea Kasenchak, Nancey Reagan, and Bill Vogler

To Ben Waldman, who taught me how to work and Lillian
Waldman, who taught me how to laugh
And to their mothers, Etta Waldman and Minny Smith,
who directly and indirectly gave to me
And to my children, Laura and David Waldman, for their
enrichment and encouragement

If I am not for myself, who will be for me?
If not now, when?
If I am only for myself, what am I?

Hillel, Sayings of the Fathers

Preface

American democracy requires citizens to make judgments about Congress and provides standards for making them. Throughout the history of Congress, both its critics and its supporters have employed democratic standards for evaluating the institution, individual members, and legislation. But different models of democracy have produced different standards, and the conflicting nature of those standards has led many people to consider one model at the expense of another or to ignore democratic considerations altogether. This book describes and analyzes congressional behavior from the perspective of two distinct models: those of adversary and unitary democracy, a framework developed by Jane J. Mansbridge in *Beyond Adversary Democracy*. Using these concepts one can better understand many aspects of congressional behavior, both those commonly discussed and those identified through this approach.

Chapter 1 introduces the adversary and unitary models and develops the framework through a case study of immigration reform proposals. The central democratic concept of representation is considered in chapter 2 through an examination of the issues of voter knowledge and campaign financing. Chapter 3 analyzes the representational differences between Congress and the president, as well as those factors that bring the two together in common deliberation. The adversary and unitary effects of congressional committees, procedures and parties, and information needs and sources are described in chapters 4 through 6. Chapters 7 and 8 employ the framework to analyze the congressional role in making foreign and economic policies. In reviewing the main ideas, chapter 9 discusses how the adversary and unitary models help us understand and evaluate legislative behavior and how both are relevant to the democratic legitimacy of Congress. Our discussion of these two models and their democratic standards of evaluation should help readers make the judgments democracy requires. By ordering information and raising new questions, this framework also makes possible a fuller understanding of Congress.

A number of factors led us to write this book. Teaching Congress courses at Wheaton and Haverford over the years has shown us what we can learn by asking important questions. Our professors in the political science graduate program at the University of North Carolina made us aware of the value of theory for both understanding and action. The American Political Science Association's Congressional Fellowship Program provided an opportunity to work with two members of great ability and clear notions of the public interest—former representative Bob Eckhardt, D-Texas, and Rep. Gerry E. Studds, D-Mass. Our experience on Capitol Hill and our knowledge of the literature on Congress convinced us of the need for a book that would explicitly link congressional behavior and democratic theory.

We are especially indebted to Jane J. Mansbridge of Northwestern University, whose work provided us with both inspiration and a framework; she also took time out from her busy schedule to discuss with us the application of her ideas to Congress. Philip Brenner of American University and Burdett Loomis of the University of Kansas read the entire manuscript in draft form and made many suggestions for improvement. Former Wheaton students Christine McLeod, Abigail Reponen, and Laurie Scully helped with some of the early research. Wheaton College and Haverford College provided support in the form of released time and a sabbatical. Joanne D. Daniels, director of CQ Press, has been an enthusiastic supporter and most helpful critic from the first stages of the project. Robert A. Feldmesser greatly improved the manuscript through excellent copy editing; Nola Healy Lynch and Susanna Spencer smoothly guided us through the editing and production stages of the book. It has been a pleasure to work with all of them. Finally, we owe special gratitude to our partners, Alice and Kay.

David J. Vogler
Sidney R. Waldman

Contents

Preface   vii

1 Congress and the Two Democracies   1
Adversary and Unitary Democracy   2
Congressional Action on Immigration Reform   5
Summary   17

2 Representation   23
Voter Knowledge   23
Campaign Financing   31

3 Congress and the President   39
Interest Representation   40
Deliberation and Governance   49
Summary   55

4 Congressional Committees   61
Constituency Committees   62
Policy Committees   66
Prestige Committees   68
Senate Committees   71
Sources of Adversary and Unitary
    Modes in Committees   73
Conclusion   75

5 Congressional Procedures and Parties   81
The House Rules Committee   81
Recording of Votes   82
Voting Cues   84

Contents

Unanimous Consent and Cloture   86
Deliberation and Debate   88
The Role of Political Parties   91
Conclusion   97

6 **Informational Needs and Sources**   101
Types of Expertise   101
The Context of Congressional Information   103
Types of Information   106
Stages of Policy Making   108
Information and the Two Democracies   113
Summary   118

7 **Foreign Policy and the Search for Consensus**   123
Congress, the President, and
   Foreign Policy   123
Consensus   127
Policy Formulation and Implementation   133
Problems and Changes in the
   Congressional Role   136
Summary   141

8 **Economic Policy and the Congressional Budget Process** 145
Budgetary Effects of Adversary Pressures   145
Options in Financing Government Programs   147
The Congressional Budget Process   148
The Use of Reconciliation   151
Net Effects of the Budget Process   155
Summary   156

9 **Conclusions**   159
Understanding Congress   159
Evaluating Congress   161
Democratic Legitimacy   164

Index   169

Congress and Democracy

Congress and the Two Democracies | **1**

Congress is, by general agreement, the most democratic of our national government institutions. The mandates of certain presidential elections and the upholding of democratic principles and procedures in certain Supreme Court decisions remind us that this democratic responsibility is shared. But it is the national legislature that lies at the heart of American democracy. James Madison's characterization of the House of Representatives as "the grand repository of the democratic principle of government" has since been extended to Congress as a whole. We see this in contemporary descriptions of the institution as the "most democratic of the three branches" and "an extraordinarily democratic body," and in the conclusion of a leading textbook that "democracy is in full flower on Capitol Hill." [1]

The concept of democracy is used to describe and explain certain aspects of the national legislature, to evaluate congressional processes and reforms, and to measure the legitimacy of the institution and the broader political system. What is not always evident in these descriptions, explanations, and evaluations, however, is the meaning given to the term *democracy*. When can we say that a member's vote or other action meets the expectations of democracy? What are the standards for evaluating the democratic effects of a congressional reform? If the concept of democracy is to be of any value to students, reformers, scholars, voters, and members of Congress, it must suggest answers to those questions and be applicable to the real world of congressional politics.

Adversary and Unitary Democracy _____

Two incidents in the second session of the 98th Congress illustrate the complexity of the concept. The first was the crucial vote on a clean air bill cast by Rep. Dennis E. Eckart, D-Ohio, in the House Health and Environment Subcommittee. On May 2, 1984, the subcommittee defeated, by a one-vote margin, provisions aimed at reducing acid rain. Representative Eckart, whose prior record on environmental issues had earned him a positive rating of 93 percent from the League of Conservation Voters, explained that his negative vote was based on concern for the economic burdens that the program would have imposed on his constituents. Commenting to a reporter that "I feel as if I pitched my tent on an anthill, there are so many people crawling over me," Eckart said that the issue was one on which "I can't win either way."

> This is how Representatives get whipsawed. I vote one way and people say, "Aren't you supposed to represent the national interest?" I vote the other way and people say, "We sent you there to represent us." It is not an easy issue. I'd just as soon not be in this position. But that's what we get paid for.[2]

The same dilemma was evident in a vote on May 16, 1984, which defeated, by 212 to 218, a defense authorization amendment that would have blocked the production of MX missiles in the following year. A Michigan State University study that was made available to members before the vote showed California, Colorado, and Massachusetts to be the states where most of the MX funds would go. For Massachusetts, the MX program would bring $2.7 billion and more than 9,000 new jobs to defense industries in the state. Yet the amendment to kill the MX program had been offered by Massachusetts Democrat Nicholas Mavroules and had been supported by every member of the state's delegation. Congressional MX supporters and defense contractors in Massachusetts criticized the delegation for voting against the interests of its constituents. In response, Massachusetts representative Barney Frank argued that legislators should not consider only the interests of the district in deciding how the federal government ought to spend money. "That is how we get in trouble," he said. Once a decision to spend money has been made, "then it is your duty to try to get as much as you can for your district. In this case we are talking about nuclear warfare. I think you have an obligation to be more cosmic in your focus."[3]

The problems raised by Representatives Eckart and Frank indicate that they weigh similar considerations in deciding how they should vote and that the relative emphasis on district and national interests will vary with the nature of the policy under consideration. There is more here than a distinction between a representative's role as a trustee acting on the basis of a long-term common interest and a representative's role as a delegate voting for district benefits. The remarks of the two legislators suggest that they see the value of both types of representation. Yet each would likely defend his own vote as being one in keeping with the premises of democracy.

Most of us are familiar with the idea of democracy implicit in Representative Eckart's vote against the acid-rain provisions. If they were perceived as leading to an increase in the already high level of unemployment in the district and to the closing of many of the area's smokestack industries, then democratic representation would seem to call for a vote against them. Does that position lead to the conclusion that the actions of the Massachusetts delegation in voting against the MX were therefore undemocratic? How does the notion of a collective representation of the national or public interest, or the common good, fit into our picture of democracy?

A first step toward answering these and other questions is to recognize that there is more than one concept of democracy and that legislators following quite different courses of action may have grounds for claiming to be acting in a democratic manner. In one concept, which Jane J. Mansbridge has called *adversary democracy,* a representative is elected by a district to protect the district's interests; different interests are equally represented in the decision-making process; there is a proportional distribution of policy outcomes (it is notable, for example, that Representative Eckart said he would have supported the acid-rain provisions if revenues from a nationwide fee on electricity were to offset the costs to Ohio industry and labor); and decisions are made by majority rule. Congressional democracy, in this view, is a bargaining process carried on by agents representing district interests, and the policy that results is a compromise that satisfies enough of those interests to produce a majority.[4]

In discussing his vote, however, Representative Eckart acknowledged that protecting the interests of his constituents was only part of his responsibility as a member of Congress. He clearly recognized the serious nature of the acid-rain problem and a national interest in dealing with that problem. Similarly, a common interest in avoiding nuclear war was a consideration that led the Massachusetts representatives to vote against what seemed to be the short-term economic interests of their districts. This gives rise to a different view of congressional democracy: *unitary democracy* (to use Mansbridge's term again), whose distinguishing characteristics are that legislators engage in face-to-face deliberation; the debate is structured by different perceptions of a common or national interest; equality of representation is of lesser concern; and conflicts are resolved by consensus or by a large majority.[5]

Three central questions arising out of this distinction serve to structure the discussion and analysis that follow in this book: How do the concepts of adversary and unitary democracy help us (1) to understand the national legislature, (2) to evaluate both the institution and its members, and (3) to judge the democratic legitimacy of the institution and the political system? While any democratic organization is likely to exhibit both adversary and unitary elements, most of our knowledge about Congress has been gathered within and explained by reference to the adversary model. Since what we find out is at least partly determined by what we are looking for, it is possible that we overlook important aspects of legislative behavior when our search is guided by only that one perspective. One goal of this book, then, is to look at Congress through the lens of unitary as well as of adversary democracy.

In addition to their effect on the description and understanding of congressional behavior, the two models of democracy have normative implications. Committee reforms that serve the adversary value of equal representation, for example, may interfere with the ability of Congress to function in a unitary way. Staff increases that permit members to better protect district interests can also decrease the incidence of face-to-face deliberation among members. Voters who judge representatives solely as advocates and protectors of district interests overlook the unitary values of conciliation and consensus-building that may help Congress solve national problems.

To illustrate both the descriptive value and the normative potential of the adversary and unitary models of democracy, this chapter will review congressional action on a major piece of legislation, the immigration reform bill. That action will first be discussed and analyzed in terms of the adversary model of democracy, the framework used in most accounts of congressional action. The chapter will then look at aspects of this case that suggest an interaction among legislators different from that of adversary democracy. This, in turn, will lead to a consideration of unitary democracy and of how that model can help explain congressional behavior and suggest additional values for evaluating congressional action. The chapter will conclude with a comparative outline of the adversary and unitary models, which will guide our consideration of some of the key elements of congressional behavior in later chapters.

Congressional Action on Immigration Reform —————————

The immigration reform bills considered in the 97th Congress in 1981-1982 and the 98th Congress in 1983-1984 were essentially the same, as were the key legislators. This is important for two reasons. First, the extended time period permitted members of Congress to exercise a wide variety of legislative skills and to hear and respond to a full range of interests on the issue. Second, much of the discussion in the 98th Congress consisted of analysis and evaluation of what had happened in the preceding Congress, presenting a picture of how the participants themselves saw Congress operating and how their behavior was affected by that perception.

On October 4, 1983, House Speaker Thomas P. O'Neill, Jr., D-Mass., announced that floor action on the Immigration Reform and Control Act of 1983 (H.R. 1510) was being indefinitely postponed. Speaker O'Neill gave three reasons for withdrawing the bill: opposition to the bill by the congressional Hispanic caucus; the fact that he could find "no constituency" in favor of the measure; and a feeling that President Reagan might veto the bill in order to win Hispanic votes in the 1984 election.[6] Rep. Edward R. Roybal, D-Calif., chairman of the Hispanic caucus, referred to the Speaker as "a profile in courage." Attorney General William French Smith, on the other hand, said that "the overwhelming majority of Americans will be dismayed by the Speaker's action," because public opinion polls showed that a majority of Americans, including a majority of Hispanic Americans, favored immigration reform. Rep. Henry J. Hyde, R-Ill., said that O'Neill's action showed that "the notion that majority rule has anything to do with the legislative process is absolutely wrong; if the Speaker doesn't want the bill to be debated or voted on, it's dead."[7] Newspaper accounts treated postponement of the bill as an example of successful lobbying in Congress, with headlines such as "Hispanic Lobby Tips Scales on Alien Issues" and "Hispanic Caucus Is Flexing Its Muscle," and descriptions such as one saying that the incident was "a classic example of how a well-organized, highly motivated lobby may, in terms of political calculations, outweigh a generalized public concern."[8]

The history of this bill had begun in the fall and winter of 1981, when subcommittees in both the House and the Senate held extensive hearings following on the recommendations of a Select Commission on Immigration and Refugee Policy and of the Reagan administration (as well as of several previous administrations). In March 1982, identical companion bills were introduced by Sen. Alan K. Simpson, R-Wyo., chairman of the Senate Judiciary Committee's Subcommittee on Immigration and Refugee Policy, and Rep. Romano L. Mazzoli, D-Ky., chairman of the House Judiciary Committee's Subcommittee on Immigration, Refugees, and International Law. In April, the two subcommittees held joint hearings on the legislation. The Senate subcommittee then quickly reported the bill out with a unanimous endorsement, the full Judiciary Committee strongly endorsed it after making some amendments, and the Senate approved the bill by an 80-19 vote in August.

Action in the House, however, followed a quite different course. The House subcommittee did report the bill to its parent committee with unanimous approval, but the full committee approved it by only a narrow margin, 15-13. Because the bill contained provisions permitting the entry of temporary foreign workers, the chairman of the Education and Labor Committee asked that his panel be given a chance to review it. Speaker O'Neill then referred the bill not only to that body, but also to the Agriculture, Energy and Commerce, and Ways and Means committees, each of which had jurisdiction over issues dealt with in various sections. The Education and Labor Committee gave the bill its approval in December, after tightening entry requirements and making other changes in the temporary worker program; the other three committees discharged it without making any changes. The Rules Committee sent the bill to the floor under a rule providing for five hours of general debate and no real limit on amendments.

The House considered the measure on Friday and Saturday, December 17 and 18. The schedule alone was enough to doom it. The five hours of debate were spread over two days, but the bill did not come up until after 10 p.m. on either day. The House was set to adjourn on the following Tuesday, and the usual last-minute rush of business before the end of the session was on. Representative Roybal had more than 100 amendments prepared for floor action; in all, a total of 300 amendments was filed. It took two hours of debate to dispose of the first amendment alone. The House had not yet voted on the bill when the 97th Congress expired, and the bill died with it.

A number of factors contributed to the bill's failure in the House. There was strong opposition by the delegations from some of the states most directly affected, and there was a shifting alliance of opposition groups that objected to particular sections. Organized labor supported sanctions against employers who hired illegal aliens but opposed the entry of temporary workers. The Chamber of Commerce and other business groups favored the temporary worker provisions but disliked the employer sanctions. Hispanic groups opposed both sections. Civil rights and religious organizations supported amnesty for aliens who had entered illegally in previous years but were concerned about problems of discrimination and civil liberties that might be associated with the employer sanctions and the procedures for identifying legal immigrants. The National Association of Counties and the National League of Cities opposed the amnesty program because of the financial burden that a consequent expected increase in welfare costs would place on local governments.

In addition to these conflicts over particular provisions, quite different assessments were offered of the overall legislation. What a proponent called "a balanced approach to the immigration problem" was described by an opponent as "a mishmash of conflicting policy decisions." [9] Before the bill went to the House floor, a Republican supporter said that "one of the problems is that everyone wants a perfect bill. The problem is there is no perfect solution." Representative Mazzoli came to a similar conclusion: "What doomed the bill was the search for perfection, and you're not going to get it.... You can't get it." [10]

But there was a note of renewal even in defeat. Representative Mazzoli was given a standing ovation on the House floor for his diligent work on immigration reform. And even though he had lost for the time being, he himself suggested that "it was very much in the national interest to have [had] long deliberation [on the issue]. Maybe that is what really is needed." [11]

In February 1983, after the opening of the 98th Congress, Representative Mazzoli and Senator Simpson introduced new legislation on immigration reform. It contained provisions for employer sanctions, amnesty, a temporary worker program, and changes in the administrative procedures for handling asylum, exclusion, and deportation. The Senate version also imposed an annual limit on legal immigration, but the House bill did not. Once again, the Senate acted quickly; in May, it passed the bill by a 76-18 vote. But for a second time, it failed in the House, when, as already mentioned, Speaker O'Neill withdrew it.

Conflicting Interests

Sen. Walter D. Huddleston, D-Ky., who had led off the subcommittee hearings in 1983, gave this explanation of the previous year's defeat of immigration reform: "In essence, the bill became mired in a morass of parochial, political, and financial self-interests that ultimately won out over the national interests." Attorney General Smith echoed that sentiment in referring to the program as "a long-term public interest effort" that "cut across a host of short-term special interests."[12] The theme of special interests also came up in testimony by Francisco Garza, a spokesman for the National Council of La Raza, a national Hispanic organization:

> ...we were very supportive of the framework of the Simpson-Mazzoli bill, because it was in our interest to compromise and negotiate with the legislators in this process, in hopes that we would win some of the aspects of the bill which we thought highly positive.
> However, as legislation moved forward ... we saw many of our interests being sacrificed, and on the Senate floor we saw a reversal of a good legalization program; it became more restricted by amendment.
> I am afraid that we have to oppose the bill with the tempered opposition that the bill is basically the same again this session, and that we fear that beyond your power, that other interests in the full Senate and the House will alter the bill such that we will face more deficiencies with this legislation.[13]

The sponsors of the 1983 bill made several changes in an effort to accommodate some of these special interests. Senator Simpson pointed out, for example, that there were some elements "which are solely there because of the response of the Hispanic community in the United States: the legalization, the increased quota from Mexico, the increased focus on the second preference, all of those things were tailored for that purpose, to respond to the Hispanic community."[14] The interests of western growers were reflected in provisions that provided for a three-year transitional agricultural labor program during which growers would be exempted from employment restrictions. The reform bill reported by the House Agriculture Committee was even more specific in addressing the interests of the growers. Declaring that the legislation before it did not "fully respond to the needs of those particular employers," the committee established a new program for seasonal workers "available only to those growers of perishable commodities as defined by the Department of Agriculture."[15]

But organized labor was not happy with this "guest worker" program. As AFL-CIO president Lane Kirkland told the Senate subcommittee:

> We are aware of the contention by agricultural employers and their advocates in the Congress that those employers, having become dependent upon a ready supply of undocumented workers, cannot now be deprived of that manpower source without being provided an alternative in the form of unlimited numbers of ... temporary workers. We cannot comprehend such an argument at a time of unprecedented unemployment and want. The AFL-CIO continues to oppose any program which would permit importation of foreign labor to undercut

the wages and working conditions of American workers. All such "guest worker" programs are contrary to the interests of American workers.[16]

The House and Education and Labor Committee responded by writing in an amendment that limited the special provisions for seasonal workers.

Another group whose interests and special concerns were raised was the American business community, as represented by the U.S. Chamber of Commerce. In 1982, the chamber had opposed the reform bill because of its employer sanctions provisions. The following year, the chamber modified its position to one of support for a sanctions program that targeted enforcement against intentional violators rather than making all business comply with extensive regulations. The chairman of the chamber's board urged the Senate subcommittee "to target those sanctions so they do not cover everybody, every employer in the United States with more than three employees. . . . We feel that the real effects there will be on small business. It will be a real burden which they do not need. We do not think the vast majority of small business is involved in the employment of illegal aliens." [17]

Business, organized labor, Hispanic groups, and western growers did not get all they wanted in the legislation that emerged, but the bill's chief sponsors clearly attempted to respond to their interests. The language used to describe the bill is replete with the terms of bargaining and compromise. Senator Simpson opened the 1983 hearings by observing that the bill was "the result of bipartisan compromise. While it is most assuredly not perfect and it will not approach perfection in implementation . . . it is a very small first step forward and contains details which obviously are not going to be satisfactory to some but, again, I say the bill represents a balanced and reasonable approach." Later, he described the bill as "delicately balanced," "a compromise of rather extraordinary proportion," and a "fragile package." A member of the House subcommittee noted that "although we were unable to please everyone, nevertheless a conscientious effort was made to accommodate diverse concerns and balance competing interests." The attorney general said that the Senate bill "represented a compromise or a balancing of [short-term special] interests." [18]

The emphasis on the bill as a product of bargaining and compromise is instructive as an indication of the values held by legislators. It is clear that a bill representing compromise and a balancing of interests is more acceptable than one that does not accommodate various interests. The language of compromise is part of the sales pitch. It is based on a conception of the legislature as a place where representatives and advocates of particular interests take part in an adversary process designed to produce compromise. That picture of Congress fits the one most often found in books and newspapers and seen in political campaigns and on the evening news.

The issue of the representation of interests came up in another way when Senator Simpson questioned whether the leaders of organized groups accurately reflected the opinions of the people they claimed to represent. For example, following testimony by representatives of the National Council of La Raza, the Mexican-American Legal Defense and Education Fund, and the League of United Latin American Citizens, Senator Simpson observed:

> We have interesting mail that comes to the subcommittee from American Hispanics, which says get off your butt and do something.... You say that you speak for them, and yet I speak with other members of the Hispanic community who are not involved with the organized groups, just like when I deal with veterans, I deal with the executive directors of veterans, and then when I go talk to veterans I find somewhat different ideas.

The senator made a similar point to a senator from California who had raised serious questions about the bill: "I think you would be interested to note that outside of California organized groups ... this subcommittee received more mail from California persons—residents, permanent resident aliens, and citizens—than from any other state, urging approval of the legislation; that we get off our duffs and do something about a problem that is very evident to all of us." [19] But it was only the accuracy of the representation, not its propriety, that was being questioned, as Senator Simpson made clear in other remarks:

> I really doubt that we will ever find or be able to generate legislative support for this legislation in California—it doesn't matter what party you are in, it can't be popular in California to resist the various chamber groups, the various grower groups, the various Hispanic groups, and certain union groups. So if I were a legislator, I would be right in there thinking that way too. I understand that totally, I really do. [20]

Thus, Senator Simpson clearly accepts the legislative process as an adversary one involving opposing interests, and he suggests that it grows out of the concern for reelection shared by all members of Congress.

Common Interests

Opposition to specific provisions of the immigration reform bill by Hispanic, labor, business, and agriculture groups clearly had a lot to do with how members of Congress voted, but there was more to congressional behavior on immigration reform than conflicting interests and constituency representation. On a number of occasions, legislators spoke about policy making in quite different terms. It has already been noted that, after the 1982 defeat of the bill in the House, Representative Mazzoli characterized the long deliberation on it as having been "very much in the national interest," and that Senator Huddleston spoke of narrow interests having "ultimately won out over the national interests." More broadly, the Senate Judiciary Committee opened its 1983 report on the bill with an extensive discussion of the concept of national interest:

> The Committee believes that the paramount obligation of any nation's government, indeed the very reason for its existence and the justification for its power, is to promote the national interest—the long-term welfare of the majority of its citizens and their descendants.
> Consequently, we believe that the formulation of U.S. immigration policy must involve a judgment of what would promote the interests of American citizens—as they are at the present time and as they and their descendants are likely to be in the foreseeable future. An immigration policy which would be detrimental to the long-term well-being of the American people should not be adopted....
> Because the well-being of individuals is affected by both economic and noneconomic circumstances, an immigration policy which serves the national interest should be based on an analysis of both the economic and the noneconomic impacts of immigration. Economic variables include unemployment, wages, working conditions, productivity, and per capita Gross National Product (GNP). Noneconomic matters include population size, other demographic phenomena, and such cultural elements as values, customs, institutions, and degree of unity or of tension between subcultures.[21]

Because elected officials almost always present their actions as being in the public interest and because of the subjective and often self-serving meanings that are given to the term, the concept of the public interest is often dismissed by political analysts. Most of the difficulties associated with the term arise when people try to clarify or define what it means. The Senate Judiciary Committee report was attempting to do this with expressions like "long-term welfare of the majority of its citizens and noneconomic impacts of policy (as well as a conditional acceptance of "charity and compassion" and "change without discomfort"). A number of questions are raised by these efforts: How long is "long-term," and of what use is the concept of "long-term welfare" to a legislator who must vote today on the basis of available information? Why is the public interest limited to the welfare of a majority of citizens instead of all citizens? What weights are to be given to the various economic and noneconomic indicators, and how are priorities among them to be determined? How does one measure the degree of "discomfort" brought about by change?

However, the concept of public interest is important to the present discussion not because of its inherent meaning, but because of its value to members of Congress. Earlier, it was pointed out that Senator Simpson and others used the language of compromise as a way of selling the bill. There was no insistence then that the senator define a "fragile package" or say precisely what is meant by a "delicately balanced" bill. Those terms are important because they have value to members of Congress, and they have value because they are associated with the notion of Congress as an adversarial institution, in which bargaining and compromise are necessary ingredients of successful decision making. The terms "national interest" and "public interest" are important to an understanding of Congress for much the same reasons. They appeal to members of Congress because they are associated with another conception of the legislature, that of a governing body acting in terms of the national interest.

Neither picture of Congress is complete or wholly accurate in itself. Congressional behavior is more than endless wars fought in special-interest jungles, and it is less than a series of leaps from one public-interest mountaintop to another. Much of what goes on in Congress lies somewhere in between. Legislative success depends partly on developing bargains among conflicting interests and partly on leading others to discover common interests. Whatever definition one gives to the public interest or the national interest, whatever its subjective meaning or ideological slant, it is based on a recognition of interests shared by legislators, their constituents, or both. The concept of the public or national interest can help us to understand Congress by leading us to a consideration of what unites legislators rather than what divides them.

What are some of the shared or common interests that members of Congress appeal to in seeking support from colleagues and refer to in describing congressional behavior? Many of them stem from similarities based either on institutional position or on support for certain fundamental principles. National legislators have overlapping interests arising out of their membership in the same governmental institution, their position within that institution, their common responsibility for governing the nation, or their representation of a broad interest that cuts across district and state boundaries. In short, they have a collective responsibility to deal with issues on the national political agenda. "Ultimately," as one member of the house has pointed out, "you have to govern." [22]

In committee hearings on immigration reform, members devoted a great deal of time to developing the idea that a serious problem existed and that congressional action was required. An example of a direct appeal to this shared interest in governing was that made by Rep. Peter W. Rodino, Jr., D-N.J., in December 1982: "If my colleagues fail to approve this bill we will send a clear message that we are unwilling to address a problem that will continue to grow and fester." [23] The same theme appeared in a question Senator Simpson repeatedly asked fellow legislators and other witnesses in the 1983 Senate hearings on the bill: "What do you foresee will occur not only in the Congress but in the country if Congress fails to do absolutely anything in this session of Congress?" [24] When Congress did, in fact, fail to pass an immigration-reform bill, it was done in a way that protected individual members from the charge that they were responsible for that failure. In 1982, no up-or-down vote was taken in the House; the bill was loaded down with over 300 amendments, brought up in the closing days of the session, and withdrawn when time ran out. In 1983, it was the Speaker who took responsibility for the House's failure to act. After the bill was withdrawn in 1982, a congressional aide admitted that "no one really wanted to see it pass," but he also pointed out that "no one wanted to be the person who stopped it." [25] This is not to say that members regularly vote for a bad bill rather than face the prospect of no bill. It is simply to suggest that members share, and are aware of sharing, a collective responsibility to govern, to propose solutions to the nation's problems.

Another aspect of the immigration reform case illustrates shared interests stemming from position within the institution of Congress. A notable aspect of the immigration reform effort was the close working relationship between the bill's sponsors, Senator Simpson and Representative Mazzoli. They organized joint hearings on the bill, traveled together around the country on the bill's behalf, and went to each other's chamber for floor debate on the bill. "Depending on how you look at it," said Mazzoli, "we're either the odd couple or the dynamic duo of immigration work." [26] Yet Senator Simpson is a conservative western Republican first elected to the Senate in 1978, while Representative Mazzoli is a moderate Democrat from Kentucky elected in 1970 and known for his strong opposition to the Vietnam War. Neither Mazzoli's district nor Simpson's state has the economic or demographic characteristics normally associated with a concern for immigration. To understand why the two men worked so well together and arrived at identical policy positions, one must realize that Senator Simpson was chairman of the Senate Judiciary Subcommittee on Immigration and

Refugee Policy and Representative Mazzoli held the same position on the House Judiciary Subcommittee on Immigration, Refugees and International Law. That shared institutional position helps account for the similarities between the two legislators and for their efforts in behalf of immigration reform. Profiles of the two men published in *Congressional Quarterly Weekly Report* in 1982 also revealed similar work styles and similar emphasis on the policy-making aspects of the job of legislator. Senator Simpson articulated a cardinal rule he followed in seeking consensus on the immigration and other bills he managed: "I never trade votes, because then you don't get one bad bill. You get two." [27] A colleague serving on Mazzoli's subcommittee mentioned that he had been particularly impressed when Mazzoli kept the subcommittee working late even though he was facing an opponent in the primary and wanted to get back to the district to campaign. "He never said anything about that," he reported. "That impressed me. That was a Boy Scout thing to do in the best sense of the word." [28]

Institutional position as a source of shared perspective was also seen in discussions of the issue of sovereignty. This issue was raised consistently during the 1983 hearings by Senator Simpson. The sole purpose of the bill, he said in opening the hearings, was "to bring immigration to the United States back under the control of the American people who exercise the first duty of any sovereign nation, and that is control of its borders." Given the focus on domestic issues in most of the deliberations, it is interesting to note that he once again referred to sovereignty in his concluding summary of the bill: "It is a bill to do one thing, one nonmystical thing, and that is to exercise the first duty of the sovereign Nation, and that is to control our borders. Bang, that is it. You can read in anything more you wish, and people do, and will, but that is the issue." [29]

Legislative consideration of the immigration reform bill also provides illustrations of how members, even when acting in their capacity of constituent representatives, may be led to common ground and a shared perspective. Indeed, when an interest is sufficiently broad to cut across a wide range of districts, it becomes difficult to distinguish national policy arguments from constituency representation. For example, some members of Congress attempted to sell Simpson-Mazzoli as a bill to increase employment. As Crewdson observed in his study of immigration policy:

> ... the substantial Democratic gains in the November [1982] elections were being interpreted by Democrats and Republicans alike as an expression of anger and frustration in a country where unemployment

was ... verging on 11 percent, and some congressmen were now talking about passing the Simpson-Mazzoli bill *without* the amnesty provision and calling it a *jobs* bill.[30]

Representative Mazzoli himself articulated this theme: "As many as one million to two million jobs would become available to Americans as a result of this bill." [31] And Senator Huddleston told the Senate subcommittee: "If we look through all the political smoke that has been generated, there is one compelling and overwhelming reason why we should pass this bill, and that is jobs." [32]

Legislators may also come to have shared or similar interests on the basis of agreement on certain ideological principles. In the adversarial view of Congress, beliefs or ideologies may give structure to the legislative battle, and immigration reform did involve a number of ideological conflicts: over civil liberties as they pertained to employer sanctions, anti-Hispanic discrimination, and identification cards for workers, and over rights to due process in admissions and amnesty programs. Differences over the value placed on such principles and ideologies can divide legislators much as conflicting interests do. But a bill can also gain support if it can be shown to be based on principles on which there is consensus. In the immigration reform case, there were three principles on which consensus was assumed: family unity, equality, and human rights.

Family unity was a value already built into immigration law. The 1965 amendments to the Immigration and Nationality Act had established seven family-based "preference" categories for the granting of visas, and unlimited entry for spouses, parents, and children of U.S. citizens. The preeminent position of family unity as a principle to be followed in any immigration reform was illustrated when Senator Simpson spoke of "sending a signal to the international community that we are continuing our commitment to family reunification," and when Father Theodore Hesburgh, the chairman of the Select Commission, said that "the number one thought that went through all of our discussions in the Select Commission was the reunification of families. This is something I think everybody can agree with. Our country is built on families." [33]

Equality and human rights were also regularly mentioned by both opponents and proponents of Simpson-Mazzoli. The concerns that many had about the impact of employer sanctions on the treatment of Hispanics were clearly based on the principle of equal treatment. The debate over amnesty for resident illegal aliens and the effective cutoff date for entry to be included in the amnesty program was often phrased in the language of equity. The director of the Washington bureau of the National Association for the Advancement of Colored People, for example, argued for amnesty up to the date of enactment on the grounds that it was "equitable" and "in the public interest." [34] Senator Simpson applauded the group for taking that position, particularly in light of the spokeswoman's admission that such a broad amnesty program would probably have a negative effect on the black employment rate. It was, said the senator, an admirable case of a group's favoring the public interest over its own interests.[35] Opponents of the amnesty program, on the other hand, also based their arguments on the principle of equal treatment, suggesting that amnesty rewarded foreigners who had entered this country illegally at the expense of those who had sought legal entry. The principle that an immigration policy should protect or advance human rights formed the basis of objections to national identity cards made by, among others, Sen. Alan Cranston, D-Calif., and Sen. Edward M. Kennedy, D-Mass. Senator Simpson also invoked humanitarian values in his opposition to temporary guest worker proposals. Guest worker programs in Western Europe developed problems, he said, when workers wanted to stay on beyond the term permitted under the program. "We asked for workers and you sent us human beings" was the senator's characterization of the humanitarian problem created by the programs of host countries.[36]

Legislative analysts may relegate the invocation of such basic values as human rights, equality, and family unity to the realm of symbolic politics, treating it as a cover for behavior that is in fact determined by a legislator's bargaining position. It is quite likely that some of the references to basic values in the immigration debate were indeed examples of such behavior. Even when that is the case, however, the use of certain values rather than others and the unifying effects of common principles on legislative coalitions make these principles worth studying. If, as Michael Malbin says, "politicians are embarrassed about basing political choices on principles of justice or 'basic values,' " or are "ashamed to acknowledge it when they debate the issues in public," [37] then we should take special notice of cases such as the debate on the immigration bill, where references to these principles abounded. These principles and values are important to an understanding of the legislative process to the extent that they are perceived as important by members of Congress themselves.

This section has shown that there was more to congressional deliberation on immigration reform than bargaining among representatives of conflicting interests. The extraordinary cooperative effort of the two subcommittees and their leaders and the nature of the arguments made in debate point to a side of the congressional process often overlooked. The predominance of adversarial, bargaining explanations for congressional behavior is at least partly due to a general acceptance of the adversary-democracy model in American society. Because Congress is a democratic institution, it is expected to act in a particular way. As the immigration reform case demonstrates, however, there are aspects of congressional behavior that seem more in keeping with another democratic model, that of unitary democracy.

Summary

Most discussions of congressional democracy focus on the relationship between members of Congress and their constituents. That is so because a key democratic link between the people and the government is congressional representation, and the primary indicator of this is policy congruence between members and their constituents. A democratic legislature, accordingly, is regarded as one in which legislators vote for policies favored by or favorable to their constituents and where there is member equality in voting. Congress is a democratic institution to the extent that its members advance and protect constituent interests in the policies that emerge from its deliberations. The model of adversary democracy incorporates this concept of government decision making as the representation and resolution of conflicting interests. The standards of adversary democracy are the most common measures of how democratic the institution of Congress is. These standards include equal representation and protection of interests, majority rule (including the associated value of accountability), and a bargaining process that produces a proportional distribution of policy outcomes. By these standards, Congress is judged in terms of its ability to resolve conflicting interests while at the same time protecting interests equally.

Unitary democracy, on the other hand, is based on a recognition that there are common as well as conflicting interests. In this model, decisions are made by consensus rather than by majority rule, and decisions are made through face-to-face contact rather than indirectly. The chief standards for measuring democracy in this sense are the degree to which common interests are perceived and acted on by decision makers and the extent to which the characteristics of the deliberative process lead decision makers to be aware of those common interests. Two important considerations are the definition of the term "interests" and the ways in which decision makers come to perceive common interests. As the term is used in this book, "interests" are the informed choices a person makes or would make among alternative courses of action. A person's interest may change from an initial preference as more information is obtained. Incomplete information may, of course, lead individuals to prefer something that is not "good" for them, and a state of perfect information is never to be found in dealing with political choices. But it is important to remember that the definition of interests being used in this book is one of *informed* choice and not simply first preferences.[38]

Just as information is always incomplete in the real world, so also it is unlikely that all people will have any single interest in common. The term "common interest," therefore, means that a relatively large number of people would make the same choice of policy among the alternatives that exist at a particular time. Mansbridge discussed three ways in which this could come about: through overlapping private interests; through empathy that leads one individual or group to adopt another's interests as its own; or through agreement on a principle (such as equality, security, or liberty) that leads people to think in terms of collective interests.[39]

The main differences between the two types of democracy are summarized in Table 1-1. Additions to this outline will be made later, but it should be emphasized here that pure forms of either type of democracy are not likely to be found in American politics. Most institutions contain both unitary and adversary elements and exhibit characteristics of one or the other model at different times or under different conditions.

It is true that Congress seems closer to the adversary model, for, as Mansbridge points out:

> Congress is explicitly designed to deal with situations where interests conflict, often irreconcilably. In situations of this kind, we cannot judge Congress according to whether or not it promotes the common interest, since no common interest exists. Instead, we must ask how it resolves conflicting interests.[40]

A similar depiction of Congress as a form of adversary democracy is found in most descriptions and analyses of the national legislature. As the discussion of the case of immigration reform made clear, however, the legislative process has many unitary characteristics as well. Mansbridge pointed to some of them:

> All parliamentary systems, for instance, end up with face-to-face meetings of elected representatives. Although the incentives to finding a common interest are usually partially offset by the personality,

Table 1-1   Two Models of Democracy

	Adversary	*Unitary*
Policy goal	Protect individual interests	Serve common interests
Focus of interaction	Legislator-constituents	Legislator-legislator
Equality of power	Necessary, to achieve equal protection of interests	Not necessary
Distribution of policy outcomes	Proportional	To public as a whole
Decision-making rule	Simple majority	Consensus or large majority
Form of negotiations	Direct and indirect	Face-to-face only

professional socialization, and structural position of the representatives, face-to-face interaction in a legislature can take on the same character as in a direct town meeting or workers' assembly. Unitary or pseudo-unitary moments in a primarily adversary system often derive from these face-to-face pressures.[41]

Analysts who employ only the adversary framework for studying Congress are likely to overlook its unitary aspects, and descriptions, explanations, and evaluations will then be incomplete. A Congress that is judged to be democratic by the standards of adversary democracy may seem undemocratic when evaluated from the perspective of unitary democracy. Reforms that enhance the ability of individual members to protect district and state interests may make it more difficult for members to perceive and act on common interests. This book is an attempt to stimulate consideration of both the adversary and unitary aspects of Congress and thus to generate fresh critical thinking about Congress and democracy.

NOTES

1. James Madison, *Notes of Debates in the Federal Convention of 1787* (New York: W. W. Norton, 1969), 39; Louis M. Kohlmeier, Jr., *The Regulators* (New York: Harper & Row, 1969), 291; David R. Mayhew, *Congress: The Electoral Connec-*

tion (New Haven: Yale University Press, 1974), 138; and Roger H. Davidson and Walter Oleszek, *Congress and Its Members* (Washington, D.C.: CQ Press, 1981), 437.

2. Quoted in Philip Shabecoff, "A Lesson From Whipsawing 101," *New York Times*, May 4, 1984, A20. See also Joseph A. Davis, "Acid Rain Provisions Cut from Clean Air Bill," *Congressional Quarterly Weekly Report*, May 5, 1984, 1009.

3. Quoted in Charles Stein, "Six Mass. Firms Play Role in Making MX Fly," *Boston Globe*, May 20, 1984, 23.

4. Jane J. Mansbridge, *Beyond Adversary Democracy* (Chicago: University of Chicago Press, 1983). By proportional outcomes we mean distributing outcomes in proportion to a group's numerical weight in the population, to the number in the group preferring that outcome or, when a good is indivisible, by "taking turns" (ibid., 30 and 265-266). Proportional outcomes as a substantive criterion of evaluation of adversary democracy and majority rule as a procedural criterion are not the same. The standard of proportional outcomes is intended to protect interests more equally than majority rule by dealing with the problem of consistently losing minorities. Proportional outcomes are an ideal that can only be approximated by political systems, never attained. Nevertheless, they are an important criterion for evaluating adversary democracy, for one can assess the degree of deviation from it. For an analysis of why proportional outcomes are preferable to majority rule as an evaluative standard, see ibid., 265-268.

5. Ibid. In this book, which was first published in 1980, Mansbridge had said that "democratic institutions on a national scale can seldom be based on the assumption of a common good" (295). In the revised preface to the 1983 edition (the text of the two is identical), she wrote, "I now think I was a bit too pessimistic about unitary possibilities on a national scale," and she added that a commitment to principle affords the most likely basis of common interests in national politics (xii).

6. Nadine Cohodas, "O'Neill Pulls Immigration Reform Measure," *Congressional Quarterly Weekly Report*, October 8, 1983, 2088.

7. All quoted in Robert Pear, "Case History: Death of a Bill/Hispanic Lobby Tips Scales on Alien Issues," *New York Times*, October 6, 1983, B9.

8. Ibid., and Steven V. Roberts, "Hispanic Caucus Is Flexing Its Muscle," *New York Times*, October 10, 1983, A14.

9. Respectively, Rep. Peter W. Rodino, Jr., D-N.J., and Rep. F. James Sensenbrenner, Jr., R-Wis., quoted in Nadine Cohodas, "Hundreds of Amendments Pose Threat to House Passage of Immigration Reform Bill," *Congressional Quarterly Weekly Report*, December 18, 1982, 3074.

10. Rep. Dan Lungren, R-Calif., quoted in Cohodas, "Amendments Pose Threat," and Representative Mazzoli quoted in Nadine Cohodas, "Immigration Reform Measure Dies in House," *Congressional Quarterly Weekly Report*, December 25, 1982, 3097.

11. Quoted in Cohodas, "Immigration Reform Measure," 3098.

12. Senate Committee on the Judiciary, *Immigration Reform and Control Act: Hearings before the Subcommittee on Immigration and Refugee Policy*, February 24, 25, and 28, and March 7, 1983, 3 and 434.

13. Ibid., 156.

14. Ibid., 226. "Second preference" refers to the spouses and minor children of

lawful permanent residents under the bill's family-reunification preference categories.

15. House Committee on Agriculture, *Immigration Reform and Control Act of 1983*, H. Rept. 98-115, pt. 2, 11 and 14.
16. Senate Committee on the Judiciary, *Immigration Reform and Control Act: Hearings*, 514.
17. Ibid., 66.
18. Ibid., 2-3, 87, 425, 30, and 434.
19. Ibid., 226 and 507.
20. Ibid., 504.
21. Senate Committee on the Judiciary, *Immigration Reform and Control*, S. Rept. 98-62, April 21, 1983, 3-4.
22. Unnamed representative quoted in John F. Bibby, ed., *Congress Off the Record: The Candid Analysis of Seven Members* (Washington, D.C.: American Enterprise Institute, 1983), 40.
23. Quoted in Cohodas, "Amendments Pose Threat," 3074.
24. Senate Committee on the Judiciary, *Immigration Reform and Control Act: Hearings*, 7. Later in the hearings, Senator Simpson provided one answer to his own question, an answer that recognized the pressure for Congress to do something when faced with a highly visible problem: "It is my humble opinion that if we do nothing, there will be the magnificent congressional knee-jerking reaction, and that will be simply to add more money to the INS [Immigration and Naturalization Service], more money to the border patrol, investigate possible use of the military, because it is such a huge border, and all that stuff" (ibid., 232).
25. Unnamed congressional aide quoted in John Crewdson, *The Tarnished Door: The New Immigrants and the Transformation of America* (New York: Times Books, 1983), 332.
26. Quoted in Nadine Cohodas, "Rep. Ron Mazzoli: Dogged Determination," *Congressional Quarterly Weekly Report*, September 18, 1982, 2301.
27. Quoted in Nadine Cohodas, "Wyoming's Simpson: Wry in the Saddle," *Congressional Quarterly Weekly Report*, June 5, 1982, 1353.
28. Representative Frank quoted in Cohodas, "Rep. Ron Mazzoli," 2301.
29. Senate Committee on the Judiciary, *Immigration Reform and Control Act: Hearings*, 2 and 229.
30. Crewdson, *Tarnished Door*, 330.
31. Quoted in Nadine Cohodas, "Prospects Brighten for Action on Immigration Reform Bill," *Congressional Quarterly Weekly Report*, December 4, 1982, 2975. In one of the few instances where there was a difference between the bill's chief sponsors, Senator Simpson opposed the characterization of the bill as one that would reduce unemployment.
32. Senate Committee on the Judiciary, *Immigration Reform and Control Act: Hearings*, 4.
33. Ibid., 137 and 151.
34. Ibid., 256.
35. Ibid.
36. Ibid., 83.
37. Michael J. Malbin, *Unelected Representatives: Congressional Staff and the Future of Representative Government* (New York: Basic Books, 1980), 234. Eric

Nordlinger's remarks are also apropos: "As a phrase, the public interest and its equivalents—the best interests of all, the common good, the welfare of the country—have evocative meanings not only when voiced on great public occasions, in speechmaking before large audiences, and in other situations allowing for rhetorical flourishes, but also in materially consequential assertions, debates, and negotiations. . . . It is the awareness of these considerations, be it conscious, dim, or subconscious, that reinforces the belief of public officials in the genuineness of their public interest preferences and the confidence that these are beneficial ones for society. In short, the public interest notion is real insofar as it has real consequences; it helps generate and reinforce divergent state preferences." *On the Autonomy of the Democratic State* (Cambridge: Harvard University Press, 1981), 36-37.
38. See the discussion of interests as "enlightened preferences among policy choices" in Mansbridge, *Beyond Adversary Democracy*, 24-26.
39. Ibid., xii, 27-28, and 72.
40. Ibid., 6.
41. Ibid., 34.

Representation | 2

The legitimacy of Congress as a national policy maker is based on representation. Descriptions of Congress as the most "democratic" of national government institutions in the United States also focus on its representational nature. Adversary and unitary democracy, however, provide different standards of representativeness. If Congress is considered in adversary terms, the primary question is whether different individual and district interests are equally protected. Consideration in unitary terms shifts the focus to representation of the common or national interest. In this chapter, such problems are addressed by looking at two factors critical to both types of democracy: voter knowledge and campaign financing.

Voter Knowledge

Both adversary and unitary democracy require knowledge on the part of the citizen. The representation of individual and district interests in adversary democracy is most likely to occur when citizens know how congressional action affects their interests and are informed about what their representatives are doing with respect to those interests. While citizens of a country the size of the United States do not engage, in any sustained way, in the common deliberation that characterizes unitary democracy, their congressional representatives do. Here, too, citizens' knowledge of the behavior both of their own representatives and of the institution is a prerequisite to proper representation in a unitary democracy. Even when members of Congress act in a unitary way, their notion of the public interest may be different from that of most citizens. Members may come to regard their own common interest as that of the people they represent. In both cases, voter knowledge and action based on that knowledge provide a corrective.

An analysis of the role of voter knowledge must of course consider evidence on the extent to which people know how well their representatives are serving both individual and common interests. But it must also look at the relationship between voter ignorance and overrepresentation of the organized, the latter being a clear deviation from the adversarial standard of equal protection of interests. It must examine the effects of members' behavior on voters' knowledge, especially in face-to-face contacts with constituents, and the limitations of those contacts. The degree to which political parties can compensate for voter ignorance and fill the representational gap that it creates must also be studied, and attention must be paid to the problem of challenger visibility in congressional elections and the effects of challengers on voter knowledge.

There is clearly a good deal of ignorance in the public's knowledge about candidates for congressional office. For example, when people were asked, "Do you happen to remember anything special that your U.S. Representative (name supplied) has done for this district or for the people in this district while (he or she) has been in Congress?" 80 percent of a national sample and 69 percent of those who had voted that year (1978) said they did not. This occurs despite the fact that representatives devote considerable resources to mailings and visits home in order to describe what they have done for their constituents. Only 29 percent of the respondents in the same survey could identify an issue of at least some importance to them from the most recent congressional campaign, and less than 10 percent could remember any bill on which their representative had voted.[1] A 1972 study showed that, while people could describe their own positions and those of both parties and both presidential candidates on questions of welfare and Vietnam, and could rate themselves, the parties, and the candidates on a liberalism-conservatism scale, a clear majority of respondents could not do the same for their congressional candidates. This was true even for those who considered Vietnam and welfare to be the most important problems facing the national government and even when they were told the party of the candidates.[2] While respondents could identify what they considered to be the most important problem facing the country and could say whether there were differences between the parties on that issue, over 60 percent could not say if there were differences between the candidates for representative in their district.[3] In 1978, over one-third of the respondents in another survey could not place their Senate candidates on a liberalism-conservatism scale on a number of issues, including the government's role in ensuring jobs and an adequate standard of living and in helping minority groups; over one-half could not do so for their House candidates.[4] Some political scientists estimate that only 20 to 30 percent of Americans fulfill the minimum conditions for issue voting.[5] It is true that even a small number of issue voters may be important in close elections, and that general findings about voters' lack of knowledge do not mean issues are unimportant in elections. Issues can have indirect effects, as when one party senses a general dissatisfaction with the state of the country and recruits and finances strong congressional challengers.[6] Nevertheless, voter ignorance does have important implications for congressional democracy, both adversary and unitary.

Consequences of Voter Ignorance

Voter ignorance raises important questions about the practice of adversary and unitary democracy in congressional politics. From an adversary perspective, we can ask how likely it is that individual interests will be protected and the power of citizens equal when there is such voter ignorance. Given what is known about general citizen dissatisfaction with Congress, it is difficult to conclude that voters ignore congressional politics because they feel their interests are being equally protected. From a unitary perspective, we can ask how likely it is that there will be a search for common interests by members and constituents, a deliberation between legislators and constituents or among constituents, when constituents are ignorant of congressional behavior.

Voters' ignorance of members has other consequences. In one study of congressional elections, 64 percent of the sample rated their representatives as doing a good or very good job and only 4 percent gave them a poor rating.[7] While Congress as an institution has received low ratings, an average of 90 percent of House incumbents and 78 percent of Senate incumbents seeking reelection have been returned to office over the past several decades.[8] An individual's representatives are often given better ratings than the president.[9] Incumbents seem to benefit from citizens' ignorance.[10]

There is another, more subtle, consequence of this ignorance. The voting public tends to focus on the president, a pattern reinforced by the media, and often holds him responsible for failures and successes on economic and other issues before it holds members of Congress responsible. Since Congress does have a major role in domestic policy, this is an important bias in public perception. As just noted, Congress as a whole is held in low esteem, yet most incumbents are reelected. Citizens apparently think the problems with Congress are due to representatives from districts other than their own, and members are apt to reinforce such views.[11] This puts the public in a curious position when a president is unable to get congressional approval of programs central to the presidential campaign. The voters blame and sometimes reject a president they have chosen, because he was not "successful," while returning to office the members of Congress responsible for his failures. If people do not appreciate the policy role of Congress and fail to hold it accountable as an institution, they will be limited in their ability to have their own interests protected or to determine whether the common interest, as they perceive it, is being pursued by Congress.

Still another effect of voters' lack of knowledge about their representatives and congressional policies is the substantial influence of intense minorities. David Mayhew refers to this as the "servicing of the organized." One might also consider it the overrepresentation of the organized, for it clearly violates the adversary standard of equal protection of interests. Because of their ignorance, constituents do not know whether their representatives are good legislative craftsmen, who can produce legislation that can effectively and efficiently achieve its stated goals, and whether they are effective mobilizers, who are interested in and able to pass legislation. Citizens also cannot readily identify "symbolic action" on the part of legislators—action that expresses an attitude but prescribes no policy effects, or the statement of policy intentions without corresponding legislation to achieve them.[12]

Many Americans sense these problems, and their feelings of impotence sometimes lead them to general distrust and skepticism, with little notion of how to remedy the situation. From time to time, they cast negative votes, usually at the presidential level. Many respond by not participating or paying attention except in the most superficial ways; they concentrate on their private lives and accept politics as unchangeable. Demagoguery, partisan rhetoric, mutual blaming, and passing the buck find this culture of ignorance hospitable. In light of their high reelection rate, so perhaps do many congressional incumbents. The consequences of voter ignorance make it less likely that interests will be protected in adversary settings or that citizens will be involved in the search for common interests in unitary settings. They also make it more difficult for citizens to determine if the common interests they see are the same as those sought by and agreed upon by members of Congress.

How Members Contribute to Voter Ignorance

There are many causes of voters' ignorance of Congress, but one that should not be overlooked here is the action of members themselves. Fenno's study of what representatives do when they go back to the district shows that they tend to play to voter ignorance by giving out general messages, such as "I am qualified" and "I am one of you and can put myself in your shoes." Members project their "qualification" in a variety of ways: showing that they are knowledgeable on the issues, identifying with the wishes of constituents, and stressing their effectiveness in Congress as reflected in seniority, committee position, or district benefits. Most voters, however, are not in a position to know if their representatives are skilled in drafting legislation or in mobilizing support for it, or what they have, in fact, accomplished in Congress. Members present these general images to win the trust of constituents.[13] With that trust, explanations of votes and other actions are less likely to be required and more likely to be believed if offered.

This raises a question about the quality of representatives' exchanges with their constituents, a question given more importance by Fenno's finding that many constituents want access, communication, and the assurance of these more than they want policy agreement.[14] Since voters often do not know what is going on in Congress relevant to them or their representatives, they settle for the promise of access. Constituents can use access to press policy claims, but if they do not know what is happening in Congress, most will not. Those who do press claims, of course, are more likely to be successful, with the result that the organized have more influence. If the adversary standard of equal protection of interests referred only to *organized* interests, then Congress would be judged in terms of its ability to produce "proportional" outcomes, or policy benefits proportional to the number of organized people seeking them. Equal protection must mean more than that, however, since not all interests, not even all intensely felt interests, are expressed.[15]

In playing to voter ignorance, members are responding to constituents as they find them and as suits their own purposes. Fenno emphasizes the importance of two-way communication back in the district, but responsiveness, accountability, and representation are not served by just any sort of communication. A member's presentation of a general image may be less useful to citizens than information permitting evaluation of the member in the light of policy ends. Access, communications, and the assurance of both are worth less to those who do not know or care enough to use them. They are necessary to representation but far from sufficient for it. Communicating has a substantive aspect not found in Fenno's descriptions. It includes telling citizens what they would be interested in "if they only knew" it had come up or was coming up in Congress; that is, communication as a form of representation.[16]

To say this, of course, is to recognize that people can have unarticulated interests. For example, when Congress increased social security taxes in 1977, it was the largest tax increase in American history. After the bill passed, members went home for the Christmas break and found a strong negative reaction to it in their districts. Had their constituents been alerted ahead of time, it is unlikely the increase would have passed. While the bill may have been in the common interest—a debatable point—the people's ability to protect their interests, as they saw them, was limited by what failed to occur before the vote. If citizens, when properly informed, still remain uninterested and apathetic, their legislators will nevertheless have fulfilled at least this part of their responsibilities.

It is easy to see why members have incentives not to tell more. The more they explain, the more they may have to explain. The more knowledgeable the voters, the more grounds they may have for criticizing their legislators.[17] The more information voters have, the higher their expectations of representatives may be. It is even possible that members believe that the legitimacy of Congress and the government might decline if legislators communicated more. Nevertheless, they arguably have an obligation to tell constituents more about why Congress does what it does. Such information might serve to sensitize citizens to the diversity of interests throughout the country, the need to accommodate those interests, and what they might want for themselves "if they only knew."

Voter Ignorance and Congressional Democracy

Fenno observes that representatives operate under certain constraints in their relationships to their constituents. They must not be too far out of line with district views (granted that such views are specific on only a limited number of issues), they must not cast a string of "wrong" votes, and they must not deviate from the voting record, commitments, and image that they have presented in the past.[18] However, these limits are too general to provide strong checks on members as they deal with issues that may be of concern to special interests but not to an ignoring, unknowing public. The public's general distrust and cynicism are blunt instruments of little use here. If anything, the cynicism actually furthers the success of many interests the public distrusts, by disillusioning people and reinforcing political inactivity.

The analysis of members' behavior in their districts raises important questions about whether the prerequisites of adversary democracy are being met, questions about the quality of legislator-constituency relationships and the likelihood of equal power and equal protection of interests. Equal power and equal protection are admittedly ideals, difficult to attain in any real adversary democracy, but what happens in the district allows a degree of inequality that does not meet adversary democratic standards. The analysis also raises questions about the attainment of some requisites of unitary democracy, particularly the quality of legislator-constituent deliberation and the "equality of respect" between legislator and constituents and between constituents themselves.[19] In a state of widespread voter ignorance, how much common deliberation and thinking about common interests can be expected?

Voters who discuss interests with their legislators, whether those interests are private or common, informed by principle or not, are a highly select group, not representative of the constituency. Of course, the limits on common deliberation by members and their constituents do not preclude members from deliberating among themselves in search of common interests. In fact, constituent trust gives members some leeway to pursue their perception of the common interest. However, when legislators do engage in such a process and come to policy agreements in Washington, the people back home are not in a strong position to evaluate whether members' perceptions of common interests are the same as their own.

As one of the conclusions of his study, Fenno suggests that members should do a better job of educating constituents about Congress instead of simply "running against it."[20] When one thinks about what that education might entail, its relevance to both adversary and unitary democracy becomes apparent. From an adversary point of view, members might explain why their efforts for a bill were defeated, or why they were unable to get all they wanted, by describing different and conflicting interests in the country. On some occasions, that might increase the legitimacy of congressional action by showing how none of the conflicting interests got all it wanted and many got at least part of what they sought. That could be a healthy concomitant of adversary democracy. In some instances, it would make citizens ask if their interests had been equally protected; in others, it would intensify conflicts that existed and reduce the leeway members now have to compromise conflicting interests in building majorities. On balance, though, both individuals and the country as a whole would probably benefit if citizens were reminded of the diversity of interests affecting congressional action. From a unitary point of view, members' explanations of congressional action might clarify the search for a common interest and the degree to which it was attained or approximated. It is probably unrealistic to expect members to engage in a great deal of either kind of explanation, since it is apparently easier and less risky for them to run against Congress. Yet some of this type of education would serve them well and benefit both the institution and the country.

Can Parties Compensate for Voter Ignorance?

One response to these problems is to argue that political parties help somewhat to fill the void created by voter ignorance. Parties do this, it is contended, primarily in presidential but also in congressional campaigns, by presenting a few major issue conflicts to the public in the attempt to win votes. Since voters get a general sense of party stances and act accordingly in elections, the winning party can implement its programs and then be held accountable in the next election. In this way, people can control what their representatives do without having to meet an unrealistic standard of citizen awareness. All voters have to do is choose between parties on the basis of those major issue conflicts.[21]

One difficulty with this contention is that it does not really describe all presidential campaigns or most congressional races. The point of greatest difficulty is when the election is over and Congress begins legislating. While some presidential campaigns come closer to approximating this model than others and some presidents are more successful in gaining congressional support, presidents often are frustrated in their attempts to achieve what they campaigned on, and the voters' "mandate" is therefore of limited value. Equally important, many significant areas of legislation are not decisively affected by the major conflicts of political campaigns. For example, many specific and important changes in the tax code enacted in the 1960s and 1970s played little part in preceding presidential and congressional campaigns, nor had the great benefits gained by the oil industry as Congress shaped an energy policy in the late 1970s been foreshadowed in presidential or most congressional campaigns prior to passage of the laws.[22]

Political parties exercise little or no control over interest groups in Congress once the election is over. Party competition in elections, therefore, does not closely control legislative outcomes. It cannot be said, then, that parties sufficiently compensate for the weaknesses resulting from public ignorance.

Effects on Elections

A closer look at congressional elections reveals differences between those in the House and in the Senate. A major finding of election studies has been the low visibility of candidates who challenge House incumbents. In one study, only 44 percent of survey respondents recognized challengers when shown their names; the comparable recognition rate for incumbents was 92 percent. In contrast, Senate challengers were recognized by 85 percent of respondents and Senate incumbents by 95 percent. Only 46 percent of the people in the survey said they had had some contact with House challengers, including mail and media contact, while 94 percent reported contact with House incumbents.[23] When asked to rate the House challenger on a scale from "very favorable" to "very unfavorable," 79 percent of the respondents had no opinion; the comparable figure for Senate challengers was 44 percent. Thus, for a large number of voters in House elections, the incumbent is known, if only superficially, and the challenger is unknown. House challengers' low visibility is also reflected in a finding that House incumbents received 66 percent of the votes of people who classified themselves ideologically opposite the incumbent (self-described conservative voters who supported a liberal incumbent, and vice versa); the comparable figure for Senate incumbents was 30 percent.[24] This low visibility of House challengers means that their potential for alerting voters to issues (whether these deal with conflicting or with common interests) and to incumbents' behavior in office goes unrealized.

Congressional election studies find very little negative voter perception of any candidate, House or Senate, incumbent or challenger. This probably reflects voter ignorance as much as anything else. A difference between House and Senate elections is that House incumbents have more control over information going to constituents than do Senate incumbents, partly due to more extensive media coverage of Senators and Senate campaigns.[25]

Campaign Financing

When one recognizes that the possibility of defeating an incumbent is the basis of legislative accountability and at the same time depends on a challenger's visibility, it is easy to see the significance of campaign financing to democratic representation. Campaign contributions pay for the polling, consultants, and media advertising of modern congressional campaigns. Studies of campaign funding show that the challenger's ability to raise funds has an important effect on the vote in congressional races involving an incumbent.[26] Incumbents, challengers, political parties, and interest groups all recognize the importance of campaign contributions, and the consequences for the political system are substantial. The average cost of a House campaign is more than $200,000 for each of the two major candidates, and many campaigns cost more than $350,000 per candidate. In Senate campaigns, the average cost per candidate is almost $2 million, and again some campaigns cost even more.

Incumbents fear well-financed opponents. Members use the resources of incumbency, such as staff, casework, mailings, visits home, voting record, and material benefits to the district, in an attempt to appear unbeatable and discourage campaign contributions to opponents.[27] Their caution in voting and in selecting issues to become involved in is related to a concern that they might stimulate strong opposition, especially well-financed opposition, at home. This caution also stems from an awareness that national party campaign organizations search for districts where the incumbent is vulnerable in order to recruit and finance strong opponents.

The efforts and actions of incumbents do not, of course, guarantee the absence of strong challengers. When such a challenge comes, incumbents must be able to mount a vigorous and well-financed response. Members' behavior even on such matters as their choice of congressional committees to serve on can be affected by a realization that they might need to raise substantial amounts of money in the future and that the clientele of certain committees would be better able to provide those funds than would the clientele of others. The great interest in serving on the House Energy and Commerce Committee in recent years has been explained by some members as a reflection of that committee's ability to stimulate campaign contributions by virtue of the issues with which it deals. Members of that committee and of the House Ways and Means Committee, which handles all tax legislation, received a total of twice the amount of campaign contributions from political action committees in 1980 and 1982 than did members of the House Judiciary and Foreign Affairs committees.[28]

Some argue that money follows votes: campaign contributors give to members with the same philosophy and policy orientation. Others suggest that votes follow money: a member's policy orientation is affected by the views of contributors. It seems most likely that both patterns of influence take place, but it is difficult to determine the extent to which each does. Either way, the influence of contributions on policy outcomes is present, and the inequality of citizen resources implies an inequality of such influence. This is not to say, of course, that campaign contributions are the only or even the most important factor influencing policy outcomes. For example, congressional lobbying, which depends on nonfinancial as well as financial resources, represents another significant influence. Nevertheless, the importance of campaign contributions in congressional elections and their relevance to both types of democracy cannot be denied.

Who are the contributors and why do they give? The largest share of campaign money for both House and Senate races comes from individual donors contributing $100 or less, followed by political action committees (PACs) and political parties.[29] PACs represent unions, corporations, trade associations, professional groups, ideological groups, and other segments of the public concerned with particular issues. Some contributors give money because they believe it will facilitate access to the member and thereby enhance their influence. As Rep. Thomas J. Downey, D-N.Y., observed: "Most issues here are not issues of conscience or morality—they are questionable calls. The people with money always have access and always have influence and are capable of tipping the scale. The whole process has become very distorted by money." [30]

That statement suggests that money exerts a deleterious influence on Congress. Just how far it can go is suggested by what Rep. Jim Leach, R-Iowa, has said: "I can remember a member coming up to me from an urban area and asking how to vote on a particular milk issue based upon what the milk lobby wanted, because he had received milk funds. I thought that was fairly ridiculous. It wasn't even his constituents' interest and he didn't even look at the merits of the bill. He looked at what his obligations were." [31] Or, as a former member of the House, James M. Shannon, D-Mass., has put it:

> We on the Democratic side ... got clobbered [in 1980], in large part because of money.... There has been all too much discussion around here about how what we do in the House and on our committees is going to affect our ability to raise money.... You go where the money is if you want to raise money, and it's not going to be with the traditional Democratic constituencies. That's the problem. That's what's feeding the ideological problem we've got.[32]

It has been suggested that the pattern of individual, party, and PAC contributions serves to "nationalize" congressional campaigns, because of the money that comes to candidates from outside the district or state. Representative Leach has described this effect in his own state:

> We're mainly rural and small business, but in elections the Republicans are largely funded by business, much of which has nothing to do with the state, and the Democrats are funded by labor, much of which doesn't have anything to do with the state. And you see a breakdown in citizen access. Not that a constituent isn't going to get in the door, but the guy who gave the money is going to get in first. So what you really see is a breakdown in constitutional democracy, which is supposed to be based on citizen access and constituency access. We're seeing regional politics and state and citizen politics become national. National groups determine outcomes, whereas local constituencies used to provide the crucial role.[33]

Yet national considerations and efforts at persuasion arising from outside a district or state perhaps do have an appropriate place in the decision making of a representative or senator. Unitary democracy, after all, requires that members be concerned with the public or national interest, with more than the district interest. Extra-district groups are entitled to participate in local campaigns, including spending money in them. The problem, according to Sen. Robert Dole, R-Kan., is that "there aren't any Poor PACs or Food Stamp PACs or Nutrition PACs or Medicare PACs." [34] That is, not all interest groups are able to contribute equal or even approximately equal amounts of money. Intense interests with ample resources, including money, are in a favored position. Consequently, to the degree that money influences legislative outcomes, the adversary standards of equal power and equal protection of interests are not met, nor is the unitary standard of deliberation about the common interest that is not biased by an unequal capacity to contribute money.

Some argue that, since money comes to congressional candidates from both labor and business, there is less reason for concern. The problem with this is not only that labor and business give unequal amounts (in total, business gives more), but that those interests do not include all relevant interests. Consumer, taxpayer, and environmental interests, for example, are not necessarily represented by labor or business. Furthermore, labor and business are not always on opposite sides. Sometimes they work together, for aid to a particular industry or for appropriations for a weapon system. Some point out that business sometimes fights business and that money supports groups that battle each other. On the other hand, competing interests sometimes carve up policy so that each wins something, with the unorganized and unfunded left out or even paying the costs. Some take comfort from the fact that candidates from both parties receive money. They feel reassured because of the philosophical and policy differences between the parties. They may point to the number of seats held by Democrats, who are regarded as less susceptible to business influence. But some Democrats also receive substantial contributions from business, contributions that will have effects on their attitudes and behavior.

In sum, from both an adversary and a unitary perspective, the representational process is flawed because of voter ignorance and the distortions introduced by campaign contributions. Widespread voter ignorance and existing patterns of campaign funding have adverse effects on equality of representation, power, and protection of interests. They also both bias and make less likely the consideration of the public interest required in unitary democracy.

NOTES

1. Calculated from data in Barbara Hinckley, "The American Voter in Congressional Elections," *American Political Science Review* 74 (September 1980): 644. Although this survey was conducted in 1978, the findings of similar studies have been remarkably consistent since they began in the 1950s.
2. Barbara Hinckley, *Congressional Elections* (Washington, D.C.: CQ Press, 1981), 101.
3. Ibid., 104.
4. Ibid., 102.
5. Ibid., 109. Hinckley points out, however, that people do not necessarily decide how to vote on the basis of these issues.
6. Gary C. Jacobson, *The Politics of Congressional Elections* (Boston: Little, Brown, 1983), 156.
7. Ibid., 107.
8. Charles Jones, *The United States Congress: People, Place, Policy* (Homewood, Ill.: Dorsey, 1982), 79 and 115.
9. Hinckley, *Congressional Elections*, 65.
10. Hinckley, "American Voter," 646. Since many of the questions asked about voter knowledge of House candidates have not been asked for Senate candidates, less is known about the latter.
11. Richard F. Fenno, Jr., *Home Style: House Members in Their Districts* (Boston: Little, Brown, 1978), 164.
12. David Mayhew, *Congress: The Electoral Connection* (New Haven: Yale University Press, 1974), 130-136. It is worth noting that not all intense interests are organized, let alone equally influential, so the representation of the organized does not mean intense views are equally represented.
13. Fenno, *Home Style*, 57-58, 84, 94, 120, and 137-138. Laslett points out that, in a "territorial society" (which, in terms of the present analysis, is usually

adversary), face-to-face deliberations among citizens cannot be the basis of political decisions. Consequently, he argues, the people must trust the face-to-face groups that rule them. Political trust thus plays an important role in reconciling a territorial society to the face-to-face groups that govern it. Indeed, the trust that legislators seek and try to foster and the apparent predisposition of many citizens to trust their own representatives may well be a response to a basic need of a territorial society; it ties a normally adversary society to its legislature. Clearly, in the United States that trust does not extend to Congress as a whole, as various studies have shown. Laslett would say that a territorial (adversary) society cannot accept as rational the face-to-face decisions of a legislature in the way the legislators do, because the citizens lack the face-to-face experience of the legislators. Peter Laslett, "The Face to Face Society," in *Philosophy, Politics, and Society*, ed. Peter Laslett (Oxford: Blackwell, 1956), 169-173.

14. Fenno, *Home Style*, 240-241.
15. One reason that not all felt interests are expressed is that the incentives for action are sometimes lacking—for example, when people think their individual activity will not make a difference in the benefits they receive. See Mancur Olson, Jr., *The Logic of Collective Action* (New York: Schocken, 1965). That benefits should be proportional to the numbers who want them is a standard of adversary democracy because otherwise, under majority rule, equal power would not give equal protection to the interests of a permanent minority. See Jane J. Mansbridge, *Beyond Adversary Democracy*, (Chicago: University of Chicago Press, 1983), 30.
16. Mail that, with the aid of computerization, members can now target to interested constituencies allows them to do more of this. A careful study of targeted mail and constituent response to it would be interesting and relevant to the issues being raised here.
17. The lower success rate of Senate incumbents may well reflect greater voter knowledge about them.
18. Fenno, *Home Style*, 151-152 and 231-232.
19. The notion of equality of respect in unitary democracy is adopted from Mansbridge, *Beyond Adversary Democracy*, 28-31.
20. Fenno, *Home Style*, 246.
21. This has been argued in an important book: E. E. Schattschneider, *The Semisovereign People* (New York: Holt, Rinehart & Winston, 1961).
22. Arthur Maass, *Congress and the Common Good* (New York: Basic Books, 1983), develops an interesting interpretation of the representational process that attempts to come to terms with the gap between the substance of citizens' decisions and the policies and implementation that eventually result.
23. Hinckley, "American Voter," 644.
24. Alan I. Abramowitz, "A Comparison of Voting for U.S. Senator and Representative in 1978," *American Political Science Review* 74 (September 1980): 638.
25. Michael J. Robinson, "Three Faces of Congressional Media," in *The New Congress*, ed. Thomas E. Mann and Norman J. Ornstein (Washington, D.C.: American Enterprise Institute, 1981), 90.
26. Gary C. Jacobson, *Money in Congressional Elections* (New Haven: Yale University Press, 1980), and Edie N. Goldenberg and Michael W. Traugott, *Campaigning for Congress* (Washington, D.C.: CQ Press, 1984).

27. Jacobson, *Money in Congressional Elections*, 122-132.
28. Elizabeth Drew, "Politics and Money: Part I," *New Yorker*, December 6, 1982, 122.
29. Jones, *United States Congress*, 100 and 129.
30. Quoted in Drew, "Politics and Money," 131.
31. "Campaigns and Deficits," *New York Times*, October 12, 1982, A24.
32. Drew, "Politics and Money," 96 and 101.
33. Ibid., 72.
34. Ibid., 147.

Congress and the President | 3

Congress and the president are institutions of both representation and governance. Both are expected to represent interests, but the electoral constituency and the interests represented by the president are different from those of members of Congress. Much executive-legislative conflict in American politics stems from those representational differences. Presidential representation is often said to be that of a broad national interest or public interest—that is, the common interest of unitary democracy. Congressional representation, based as it is on district and local interests, reflects many of the attributes of adversary democracy. Thus, the concepts of unitary and adversary democracy give us a fresh perspective for examining executive-legislative conflict.

As institutions of governance, Congress and the president are responsible for developing national policies. While a president or a member of Congress might act independently in representing interests, the Constitution requires joint action in governing. Descriptions of joint action in most accounts of Congress and the president fit within the framework of adversary democracy. Presidents are said to win approval of economic programs or defense systems by assembling majority coalitions of diverse interests. While such descriptions accurately indicate the basis of governance in many cases, there are other ways in which presidents and Congress get together and other grounds for policy agreement. Unitary democracy's process of consensus building through deliberation is one such alternative, and that concept will be employed in this chapter to better understand Congress and the president as together they exercise the powers of governance.

Interest Representation

It is, as the *New York Times* has said, a "political truism" that presidents are expected to represent the national interest and members of Congress to represent local interests. The *Times* used the term in an editorial criticizing two senators who were running for the presidential nomination in 1984, because of their opposition to the immigration reform bill (see chapter 1).

> If you were a senator from California or Colorado, with many Hispanic constituents, you might well be hesitant about a bill that several Hispanic organizations oppose. But Senators [Alan] Cranston and [Gary] Hart are running for President. If they're truly interested in demonstrating their national perspective, let them get out of the way.[1]

This representational distinction is one often made by presidents. Thomas Jefferson, for example, implied that presidents have an advantage over those "whose positions will not command a view of the whole ground," and he urged members of Congress not to "condemn what they would not if seen in all its parts." Woodrow Wilson observed that the president's voice "is the only national voice in affairs. . . . He is the representative of no constituency, but of the whole people." John F. Kennedy echoed this thought: "Only the president represents the national interest."[2] Such statements are not surprising, since a president benefits from the belief that Congress represents local interests while the president the national interests.

Members of Congress tend to accept their role as representatives of local interests. One put it this way, quite bluntly:

> My first duty is to get reelected. I'm here to represent my district. This is part of my actual belief as to the function of a Congressman. What is good for the majority of districts is good for the country. What snarls up the system is these so-called statesmen—Congressmen who vote for what they think is the country's best interest.[3]

One House member seemed to arrive at much the same conclusion, though perhaps a little more reluctantly: "While we are here first and foremost to represent the national interest, and while I'm a firm believer in that, nevertheless you have to look out for the interest of your people." An extreme statement of this local orientation was that made by a representative to some disguised FBI agents during the Abscam operation. Washington, he said, was a "big pie," and "each member is sent there to bring a piece of that pie back home."[4]

Scholars, too, regularly point to this difference between the president and Congress, as the following excerpts from social-science works show:

> ... both president and Congress respond to the wishes of the public (and they both do so more frequently than they are given credit for). ... In the degree to which they prefer *national* interests, however, there is a significant distinction. Members of Congress represent different publics, different from each other's and from the president's. Their constituencies vary widely, [while] the president's constituency consists of all the people. ... The consequence is that there are consistently some differences between the policy positions of Congress and those of the president.
>
> Every member of Congress depends for reelection on constituency-based political forces. Thus different members speak for different economic, social, and geographic interests, and all members are necessarily somewhat parochial at times in their policy orientations. ... In contrast, the president's constituency is the entire nation. The president alone can speak authoritatively on behalf of the national interest.
>
> In conflicts between the branches, the executive appears, usually, to reflect the *national* interest, the legislature the *local* or *special* interest. ... The executive branch tries to consolidate or eliminate small and inefficient hospitals, research stations, post offices, and Amtrak schedules, and the legislature resists. ... The executive tries to limit the diffusion of model cities, and the legislature finds it necessary to extend the benefits until most of the 435 congressional districts receive a share.[5]

Sources of Conflict

This fundamental difference between the two branches is bound to produce conflict, both between Congress and the president and among legislators acting in behalf of their constituents. It constitutes, in effect, an "invitation to struggle." [6] The sources of conflict lie in institutional differences in the nature of constituencies, internal structure, and information and expertise.[7]

Constituencies. Efforts to explain what it is that draws a president to give primacy to national needs and legislators to local interests have taken two forms. The first is a simple electoral explanation. To win election, a president must build a broad national coalition. The relative importance of particular states and sections will vary, but a president's constituency is essentially a national one. This "whole-nation constituency" is not the same as the total congressional constituency of 435 districts and 50 states. The different lengths of terms mean that only a third of the senators stand for election in a presidential year and that all House members must face the voters in midterm as well as presidential-year elections. Changing economic and political conditions, in effect, produce changing constituencies over the course of those electoral years. Even in a presidential election year, an interest of great electoral importance in a congressional district may be of little importance nationally. An additional factor making for different constituencies is the overrepresentation of rural interests in the Senate and urban interests in the electoral college. So the constituency of the president is not simply the sum of House and Senate constituencies.

On the other hand, some observers have suggested that the important difference between the presidential constituency and the congressional ones is the greater heterogeneity of the former. For example, former representative Bob Eckhardt of Texas, when asked why the president "would not have to respond to the same kind of localistic and particularistic pressures which move and must move" members of Congress, replied: "I think he is equally acted upon, but he is acted upon by so many divergent and interrelated interests that he must necessarily reconcile these interests in favor of a common interest." [8]

The effects of constituency size and of the corresponding degree of diversity were central to McConnell's analysis of American politics. Narrow geographic districts, he argued, are more likely to be dominated by a single or a few economic interests. A broader constituency will include more competing interests, which serve to check one another, and it will also include the types of interests "most commonly called 'the public interest.'"

> Active support for such interests must come from relatively small numbers of people with some sense of cause and dedication. These numbers . . . may have no effect in small constituencies and, if they are to succeed, must have the larger numbers of a big constituency from which to draw enough people with the time, money, and drive to work for a cause the benefits of which will be shared by all.[9]

Because the president responds to a broader, more heterogeneous constituency than do members of Congress, this argument goes, his policy goals are more likely to reflect the wider values of the public interest. The checking of interests within a heterogeneous constituency in effect "liberates" the president; the scope of his constituency makes the diffuse "public interest" relevant.

It is important to recognize that there are great variations in the constituencies of different members of Congress. Although the districts of House members have roughly equal populations, they vary a great deal in degree and type of cultural, social, ethnic, and economic diversity. There are still greater differences among senators' constituencies: Alaska's two senators, for example, represent less than half a million people, while California's represent more than twenty-three million. Because Senate constituencies are on the whole larger and more diverse than those of House members, and therefore more closely approximate the presidential constituency, McConnell hypothesized that the Senate could be expected "to serve general interests" more often than the House.[10] There is some evidence that senators' positions tend to be closer to the president's than representatives' positions are, but the overriding influence of party affiliations precludes a general statement that the Senate supports presidential programs more often than the House does.[11]

Since House districts do differ in degree and type of diversity, there should also be differences in the weight which House members place on broad national interests. Constituency diversity is a difficult variable to measure, but it has been used in studies of electoral competition. While there is some support for the hypothesis that diverse constituencies will produce more competitive congressional elections than homogeneous constituencies, the relationship is not a strong one and does not apply at all for some time periods.[12] These studies do not bear directly on the question of constituency diversity and legislators' decision making. Fenno's study of a selected group of representatives led him to conclude: "Of all the internal characteristics of the district, the one that best illuminates subsequent member perceptions and behavior is district homogeneity or heterogeneity." [13] Fenno studied the different ways that representatives presented themselves to constituents, how they allocated their time and resources between Washington and their home district, and how they explained their Washington behavior to constituents. Their perception of the diversity within their district affected all three of these elements of their "home style." Representatives from heterogeneous districts, for example, were found to have greater latitude in choosing how they would present themselves to constituents than did those from homogeneous districts.[14]

Fenno's work suggests that the thesis regarding the effect of constituency heterogeneity on the consideration of broad interests is not limited to the distinction between the president and Congress. The constituency of no single House member or senator, of course, comes close to the size, scope, and heterogeneity of the president's constituency. But some studies of Congress offer a heterogeneity explanation for congressional behavior that is markedly similar to that offered for presidential behavior. A major study of trade policy, for example, concluded that representatives "feel much freer than most outsiders think," and it employed a diversity explanation for that leeway:

> Paradoxical as it may seem, their "freedom" comes from the excessive demands made on them. The complexity of their environment which seems to congressmen to rob them of initiative thrusts initiative back on them, for, when the demands on a man's resources clearly exceed his capacity to respond, he *must* select the problems and pressure to which to respond.[15]

Arthur Maass made a similar point in discussing the drawbacks of proportional representation (PR) for selecting legislators: "Under PR, the constituency of each representative is so homogeneous that representatives have little room to focus on the broader public interest and to exercise the discretion that should be theirs if the legislative and administrative processes are to fulfill their responsibilities." [16]

In sum, while the institutional perspective of the president is different from that of a member of Congress, and while some of that difference can be attributed to the relative size, scope, and complexity of their constituencies, the heterogeneity thesis can also be applied, to some extent, to explain the behavior of members of Congress. More will be said about the notion of congressional "parochialism" later in the chapter.

Internal Structure. Another reason often cited for conflict between the president and Congress is the difference in the organizational structure of the two institutions, though this, too, is related to the character of representation. The centralized hierarchy of the executive branch creates a system of interest representation different from that provided by the decentralized Congress. Edwards has described the difference in the following way:

> The executive branch is hierarchically organized, facilitating the president's examining a broad range of viewpoints on an issue and then weighing and balancing various interests. This structure also helps the president to view the trade-offs among various policies. Since one person, the president, must support all the major policies emanating from the executive branch, he is virtually forced to take a comprehensive view of those policies.
>
> Members of Congress frequently do not take such a broad view. Each house of Congress is highly decentralized, with each member jealously guarding his or her independence and power. . . . While the structure of Congress ensures that a diversity of views will be heard and that many interests will have access to the legislative process, it does not follow that *each* member will hear all the views and see the proponents of each interest.[17]

In addition, assignments to congressional committees produce weighted representation on certain panels (westerners on the Interior committees, commodity interests on Agriculture), and the increasing importance of subcommittees further encourages member specialization. In making the hundreds of individual voting decisions that come up in each session, legislators rely on the cues of other members whose general views they share, rather than undertaking a comprehensive analysis of their own. The policies that emerge from such a structure, at least some of the time, are policies that Congress as a whole has ratified after listening to some interests more than others. The organization and structure of Congress produce a restricted and biased representation of interests compared to that of the executive. As Edwards suggests, "the different structures would not necessarily lead to a divergence of viewpoints between the president and Congress if the people who influenced the votes of each legislator represented the full range of views in the chamber, but they do not." [18]

There is no doubt that the legislative cue network filters information; to provide a cue taker with the full range of positions and supporting information on an issue would undercut the very reason for having a cue network in the first place. There are two characteristics of legislative cue taking, however, that modify its biasing effects. The first is that legislative experts, the initial cue givers, provide a link between legislators and extra-legislative experts from the executive branch, academia, the media, and interest groups. A cue network that seems limited and restricted from the viewpoint of the person receiving those cues, from the inside looking out, may in fact allow for relatively broad representation.[19] The second is that legislators do not make policy decisions *de novo*. Most issues have been around for a long time. Most bills have come up before. The recurring nature of issues and legislation means that members of Congress have a decisional base already in place and are open to influence primarily at the margins. Rather than simply repeating old arguments, lobbyists and colleagues who seek to change votes would seek to provide new information and new points of debate. Over time, this gives legislative policy making a breadth and scope beyond that seen in the vote on any particular bill.

Furthermore, while few would deny that the executive branch is more of a centralized hierarchy than the legislative, the contrast can be overdrawn. The process of policy choice and policy implementation within the executive bureaucracy, as described by Neustadt and others, shares many of the characteristics normally ascribed to the legislative process: power exercised through persuasion rather than command;

authority based on information; and bargaining and reciprocity. The restrictions and biases that develop in the information network of most administrations produce real limits on "the president's examining a broad range of viewpoints on an issue and then weighing and balancing various interests." The presidency today is more likely to be described as "fragmented" than as the peak of a clear hierarchy. Some national interests are represented better than others in executive decision making. In short, the internal structure of the executive branch exhibits some of the same characteristics, limits, and biases that are more often attributed to the legislature.[20]

Information and Expertise. "Despite the substantial increase in congressional staff in recent years," Edwards has pointed out, "members of Congress rarely have available to them expertise of the quantity and quality that is available to the president," and the result is not just that Congress and the president see issues from different perspectives, but that "the president's views will generally be buttressed with more data and handled more expertly." [21] One reason for this is the great difference in the numbers of people working in the executive and legislative branches. Congress employs about 32,000, the executive almost 5,000,000. In addition to size, the executive benefits from a career civil service, centralized recruitment and hiring, and employment requirements of technical expertise. Members of Congress, as a result of these differences, are said to have less information and a lower quality of information than do executive policy makers.

Nevertheless, the sheer volume of information that is available to members of Congress is staggering. There are times, of course, when members of Congress contend that they have been denied essential information. Sen. Daniel Patrick Moynihan, D-N.Y., resigned for a short period in 1984 as vice-chairman of the Senate Intelligence Committee on the ground that vital information on the mining of Nicaraguan harbors by the Central Intelligence Agency had been illegally withheld from the committee. Normally, however, a lack of information is not the problem. One representative has said: "The real information difficulty I have is the frustrating knowledge that I have that everybody would like to educate me more than I am able to absorb." A senator has made a similar complaint: "I have too much information. There is no scarcity of any information that I've found on any of my committees. I can't keep up with all of the material that is readily available." [22] If Congress does have an information disadvantage vis-à-vis the executive, it may not lie in the volume of information available.

But too much information can have the same effect as too little. Without some way to order and interpret the vast amount of information they do have, members of Congress would again be at a disadvantage. The real difference between Congress and the executive may lie in the latter's greater capability for ordering information, for improving its quality, and for making it relevant and accessible. When he was a member of the Senate, former vice-president Walter Mondale had this to say on the subject:

> I have been in many debates ... that dealt with complicated formulas and distributions. And I have found that whenever I am on the side of the Administration, I am surfeited with computer print-outs and data that comes within seconds, whenever I need it to prove how right I am. But if I am opposed to the Administration, computer print-outs always come late, prove the opposite point, or always are on some other topic. So I think one of the rules is that he who controls the computers controls the Congress, and I believe that there is utterly no reason why the Congress does not develop its own computer capability, its own technicians, its own pool of information.[23]

By 1984, Congress had an annual budget of $34 million for the House Information Systems and the Senate Computer Center. In addition to providing assistance in the areas of office administration, constituent casework, and public opinion, congressional computers permit personal and committee staffs to conduct research on pending issues. When the president submits his budget to Congress, it is now accompanied by a computer tape of the budget, which permits independent analyses by committees and agencies of Congress. A decade after Senator Mondale had made his observation, Sen. Charles McC. Mathias, Jr., R-Md., expressed the opinion that "in some ways, I don't think Congress could have survived as a meaningful institution without the computer," for without it, he said, "we might have drowned in a sea of information." Even more pointed was the remark of a former staff member of the Joint Tax Committee: "Giving Congress the ability to use the analytical ability of the computer has worked to equalize the power of the executive and legislative branches."[24]

Even with these changes, the different information systems and perspectives of the two branches continue to affect the relations between them. But the information gap has been narrowed, and we can no longer assume that a president's views will be "buttressed with more data and handled more expertly." (See chapter 6 for a further discussion of the role of information in policy making.)

The Charge of Congressional Parochialism

Although there is a widespread belief that Congress has a local or parochial cast to it, in contrast to the more comprehensive national perspective of the president, evidence in support of this belief is not readily available and the reasons offered for expecting it to be so are not convincing. The argument of constituency heterogeneity seems to overlook the diversity that can be found in legislative districts as well. The explanation in terms of internal structure paints a picture of centralization and hierarchy in the executive branch that is questioned by current scholarly work on the presidency. Differences in information and expertise have been mitigated somewhat by laws mandating that the executive provide Congress with information and by an increase in the legislature's capacity for processing information.

In a study conducted in the early 1960s, Davidson interviewed 87 members of the House and asked them, among other things, about the relative importance they assigned to district and national interests. While 42 percent did say that the interests of their district were their dominant concern, 28 percent said that national interests dominated and 23 percent said that they gave equal importance to district and national interests.[25] Davidson concluded that his study supported the thesis that "legislators are more frequently parochial than national in constituency focus," but only with "important qualifications"—namely, that some members were aware of policy concerns that transcend district lines, criticized the parochialism of their colleagues, did pay attention to the recommendations of national policy experts, and had ties to national and institutional constituencies.[26] Brenner, commenting on this study, went further: "The surprise here is how large a group Davidson found that was willing to express a non-local focus, because members tend to cultivate a local twang even when they address international problems."[27]

The primary concern of members of Congress for their own reelection has become an established part of the literature on Congress,[28] and it has frequently been asserted that this concern impels legislators to stress both legislative and nonlegislative activity that provides local benefits. Nelson, for example, has written:

> Personal ambition and constituents' demands powerfully influence how members of Congress behave in office. Most channel their energy and resources into activities that translate readily into votes. This creates an anomaly: although Congress's main constitutional task is to legislate in the national interest, most of the activities that produce

votes for members are nonlegislative, primarily "pork-barreling" and casework.[29]

Nelson cited a public-opinion survey conducted in 1977 for the House Commission on Administrative Review, in which voters were asked whether they thought that their representative "should be primarily concerned with looking after the needs and interests of 'his own district' or 'the nation as a whole.' They chose 'own district' by a margin of 57 to 34 percent." [30] Remarkably, however, when, as part of the same survey, members of the House were asked a similar question, 45 percent said they were "primarily concerned with looking after the needs and interests of the nation as a whole," while only 24 percent said they were "primarily concerned with looking after the needs and interests of their own districts." [31] Since this survey was made 13 years after Davidson's, it appears that Congress—or at least the House—is a less parochial institution than it once was.

The studies cited so far deal with the attitudes of legislators rather than with their behavior. When the votes of members of Congress are examined, the parochialism thesis is further weakened. Arnold's analysis of the composition of federal expenditures from 1950 to 1980 led him to conclude:

> The notion that federal expenditures are increasingly shaped by congressional competition over local benefits is inaccurate. [Actually, there has been] a relative decline in the volume of particularized benefits: water projects, project grants, construction and staffing of federal facilities, and procurement contracts all have been declining in relative magnitude.... They have been displaced by the growth in formula programs (such as revenue sharing) and entitlement benefits for individuals (such as Medicare). These newer programs deliver benefits as a matter of right, not privilege, and congressmen have fewer opportunities to claim responsibility for them.[32]

At the very least, then, the belief that legislators rank district interests above national interests does not rest on a firm empirical base. That members of Congress are concerned with district interests goes without saying. But to generalize from that to an assertion of institutional parochialism is not justified on the basis of current data.

Deliberation and Governance

Most discussions of local and national interests assume they are unavoidably in conflict. If Congress represents district interests, it is difficult or impossible for it to act in the national interest. Conversely, the national perspective of the president overrides his awareness of and ability to respond to local concerns. Pitkin has criticized scholars for being "far too ready to accept this as a true dilemma, with mutually exclusive alternatives," and she suggests a way to resolve it:

> It would be useful to distinguish between what we might call initial-interest-claim, on the one hand, and final-objective-interest, on the other. The initial-interest-claim of a locality or group can be and often is opposed to the initial-interest-claim of the nation. But the nation also has an interest in the welfare of its parts and members, and they have an interest in its welfare. So, in theory, for each case there should exist an ideal final-objective-interest settlement (whether or not we can agree on it), giving just the right weight to all considerations. . . .
>
> Politics entails the reconciliation of conflicting claims, each usually with some justice on its side; the harmony of final-objective-interests must be *created*.[33]

From this point of view, representation can be seen as a process moving toward a settlement or a policy resolution, and the process is more than a recognition of initial interests: it is the creation of a shared interest in national policy. Recasting the conflict between district and national interests in this way changes our understanding of the relationship between Congress and the president. It leads us to ask whether the interaction between the two is not sometimes a joint search for policies in the public interest, rather than always being a negotiation between institutions with different interests. Instead of focusing on what pulls the two institutions apart, we need to turn our attention to factors that contribute to executive-legislative deliberation and agreement.

Bessette has defined a deliberative institution as "one in which the members reason together about the problems facing the community and seek to promote what they judge to be good public policy. In the United States Congress, then, deliberation is a process of reasoning on the merits of public policy. It includes activities like the investigation and identification of social needs, the evaluation of ongoing programs, the formulation of legislative remedies, and the consideration of alternative proposals." [34] The process of deliberation, as he has noted elsewhere, is not limited to the internal workings of Congress. At least a part of the regular interchange that takes place between the president and Congress is deliberation and debate on the merits of alternative public policies.[35]

Elections

At first blush, the electoral connection between the president and Congress appears to be a rather tenuous one. Incumbent members of the

House in particular enjoy an electoral advantage that helps to insulate them from national trends, since the great majority of those who run for reelection are reelected. The ability of presidents to affect the outcome of House and Senate races, to pull supporters into office on their coattails, has declined to the point of disappearing over the last decade. Rather than being referenda on the policies of a particular administration, congressional elections are now seen as contests between local forces. Mann, for example, has argued on the basis of his study that "congressional elections are local, not national, events: in deciding how to cast their ballots, voters are primarily influenced not by the President, the national parties, or the state of the economy, but by the local candidates." [36] Other scholars, analyzing both aggregate voting data and survey data, agree.[37]

However, interpretations of congressional elections depend to some extent on the question being asked. Is an effort being made to understand why Democrats received 56 percent of the national vote for House candidates in 1982? Or how the Republicans maintained control of the Senate in 1984? Or why one particular candidate defeated another particular candidate in a particular district? Those are three distinct questions.[38] Mann's concern was with the last of the three. Jacobson, on the other hand, was interested in explaining congressional elections as a collective choice being made by the voters across the nation, and because his focus was different, he arrived at a different conclusion about the importance of national forces in these elections:

> For now, at least, although national issues may not count a great deal in individual voting decisions, they do influence the strategic decisions of congressional elites. Elite strategies generate choices across states and districts that systematically reflect national forces. Responding to candidates and campaigns, voters respond systematically, if indirectly, to national forces as well. Collectively, congressional elections hold the administration's party responsible for the general state of economic and political life.[39]

What matters most about congressional elections, however, is how political leaders perceive them, for it is their perceptions of the election process that will determine their behavior. Although studies of those perceptions consistently show members' awareness of the electoral rewards for constituency service and their attention to district concerns, they also reveal a national, "presidential" component in members' understanding of what wins elections. The belief of many members in a policy mandate growing out of the 1980 election, for example, has been used by scholars to explain the early victories of the Reagan administration in Congress, just as they later used members' ideas about a "lost mandate" to account for its lack of success after the 1982 elections.[40] Or, in the words of a freshman representative elected in the latter year: "People in the class of 1982 feel they were elected largely over a disastrous economic policy, and most of us came here fairly serious about doing something about that." [41]

In short, it does seem that elections provide a common frame of reference for the president and members of Congress. Even with the intensified partisanship and conflict that an election brings, he and they are likely to be talking about the national issues that they all consider electorally important. In doing so, they are in effect engaging in activities associated with deliberation: identification of social needs, evaluation of programs, formulation of legislative remedies, and presentation of alternative proposals. The shared framework of an election brings them together, even if for conversation more than for conversion.

Vetoes

A veto is explicitly a negative act. It would seem to indicate a breaking off rather than a continuation of joint effort. That might be an accurate picture had the veto power provided for in the Constitution been absolute, a possibility explicitly rejected by the Philadelphia convention.[42] But the veto power is not absolute. Article I requires that a president inform Congress of his "objections" to a bill when he returns it to them after a veto, and that Congress make note of such objections and reconsider the bill. A two-thirds vote in both chambers can then make the bill a law without the president's signature.

The Constitution makes no provision for a legislative veto. Nevertheless, the legislature has come to exercise a veto through laws that prohibit particular executive actions without congressional approval or that demand an end to executive action. Although there are different forms that the legislative veto can take, a congressional resolution that includes reasons for the action is the most common instrument. Like the "objections" that accompany a presidential veto, the reasons given for a legislative veto can serve as a basis of dialogue between the president and Congress.

If the only purpose of a veto were to uphold the separation of powers—to protect the executive from legislative encroachment and vice versa—then an absolute veto would suffice. But the additional elements in the veto process—the statement of objections, the reconsideration, the possibility of override—suggest an additional purpose. As Bessette has put it: "The clear intention of this process was to raise the conflict above a battle of wills to a genuine contest of opinion and argument. Both the actual and threatened use of the veto will foster a kind of deliberation *between* the branches of the government."[43] Interpretations of the legislative veto often include similar observations. Vetoes, and the much more common threat of a veto, are a form of legislative-executive conversation. They produce negotiation and compromise, deliberation and shared solutions more often than they do deadlock. When the U.S. Supreme Court declared unconstitutional one form of the legislative veto in its *Chadha* decision of 1983, both the majority opinion of Chief Justice Warren E. Burger and a dissenting opinion by Justice Byron R. White discussed the legislative veto within the context of deliberation.[44]

The Budget

Prior to the Congressional Budget Act of 1974, the budgetary process was a disjointed one. The executive budget both served to assign priorities in support for government programs and was also an instrument of fiscal policy. Taxing and spending proposals in the president's budget were aimed at sustaining controlled economic growth. The congressional budget, on the other hand, was the total of all the separate appropriation decisions made for that fiscal year, offset by tax revenues. Congress did not respond to the president's overall program; rather, it made a series of independent decisions about levels of spending for particular areas. The autonomy of committees, the division of labor, and the specialization that characterized Congress precluded any overall consideration of budget policy. Spending decisions were made independently of taxing decisions, and levels of spending on particular programs or sectors were determined without reference to overall levels of spending. The lack of a mechanism for budgetary policy making in the legislature consistently led to higher levels of spending than those called for by the fiscal policy of the president. Battles between a Republican president and a Democratic Congress greatly politicized this difference in the early 1970s.

The Congressional Budget Act of 1974, in effect, created the budget process that had been missing in Congress. Budget committees were established in each chamber; the functional budget categories already used in the executive branch were adopted for Congress; a Congressional Budget Office was created to provide independent budget analysis; and Congress was required to vote on overall spending goals and actual spending totals in the form of budget resolutions. This law changed the relationship between Congress and the president. A leading student of the budgetary process, who helped to write the act, has said about the change:

> Although the congressional budget process can be a competing power center, it also provides a forum for considering the president's budget "whole" and on his terms. It provides a structure whereby congressional leaders can negotiate with White House officials, reach an agreement, and move it through the House and Senate. This was the way the process worked in March 1980 when the Carter administration and a congressional delegation formulated a revised budget.[45]

The area of budgetary policy making nevertheless continues to be one of great conflict between the president and Congress. The 1974 reform has in some ways increased rather than reduced the level of conflict, but the debate is now more focused. Congress now speaks the language of fiscal policy, of proper levels of total spending, of deficits, of areas where budget cuts are needed. The debate between the president and Congress on budgets has become a debate over national policy.[46] (The budget process will be considered further in chapter 8.)

Ideology

The concept of ideology is often used in describing the presidency, Congress, and the interaction between the two. In a recent book on the Reagan presidency, Greenstein suggests that "no other president has come to office after a remotely comparable prior career of making public an ideologically consistent (if very general) commitment to a political philosophy." When Speaker O'Neill pulled the immigration reform bill from the schedule in 1983, Senator Simpson responded by saying that he would "rely on those of [O'Neill's] own political ideology to be telling him how he misfired this round." And Lawrence O'Brien, who directed congressional liaison for Presidents Kennedy and Johnson, wrote this about his experience:

> Sometimes in my mind's eye I saw two great armies facing one another across a vast field of battle. One army—our army—was led by the President and included in its ranks the forces of organized labor, the urban political leaders, the emerging black political spokesmen, and many of the nation's intellectual luminaries.
>
> Ours was a formidable force, and yet facing us was a no less powerful legislative army led by such Republican stalwarts as Ev Dirksen and Charlie Halleck, backed by the vast resources of the American business community, the major corporations and especially the oil industry, as well as the medical profession, and important segments of rural and suburban America.[47]

Ideology can clearly be a source of conflict between the president and Congress, especially in the form of a conflict between liberalism and conservatism. But ideology can also refer to belief systems and values that are accepted by most of the political leaders in a society. Huntington, for example, has written about the core political values of liberty, equality, individualism, democracy, and rule of law, which form the basis of his version of the American Creed.[48] Although not strictly an ideology in the sense of establishing priorities among different values, this set of core beliefs does provide a common reference for deliberations among political leaders in society.

A shared belief system that does serve as an ideology in the establishment of priorities is capitalism. Wolfe has shown how the expansion of presidential power in this century has been closely tied to the revitalization and expansion of American capitalism.[49] Brenner has discussed the way in which the dominant ideology of capitalism structures the interaction of Congress and the president.[50] Disagreements and debate between the president and Congress take place within the broad agreement reflected in the shared ideology of capitalism. Not only do members of Congress and the president share this ideology; they also have a stake in maintaining the legitimacy of Congress and the presidency as institutions, and that legitimacy is itself based on maintaining the dominant ideology of capitalism.

Summary

Legislative-executive conflict is generally explained in terms of representational differences. Congress and the president represent different constituencies, and that is what lies at the heart of most interbranch conflict. Such an explanation fits best with the adversary model of democracy. To understand congressional behavior and public policy, we look to the different interests of voters and particular groups. Congress, in this view, is an intermediary for translating the demands and interests of societal groups into policy. The chief question to be asked is how well the institutions of government represent the demands and interests of all people in society.

More is required of political leaders than representation, however. Congress and the president must also govern. In Fenno's words, "Representative government requires more than accountability and responsiveness to constituents. It also requires the governing of constituents." Similarly, Pitkin speaks of the "dual task" of the representative as "both special pleader and judge, an agent of his locality as well as a governor of the nation. His duty is to pursue both local and national interest, the one because he is a representative, the other because his job as representative is governing the nation." And Brenner writes of the way in which "members come to see themselves as rulers of the country" through their collective experience as legislators.[51]

When members of Congress interact with the president on the basis of this shared responsibility for governing, they do so in ways that seem closer to unitary than to adversary democracy. Legislators and the executive share the experience of governing, as well as the information and the awareness of a wide range of options, which can lead them to *create* policies perceived to be in the public interest, rather than merely responding to the policy preferences of societal groups. The act of governing, in other words, *generates* policy preferences and interests just as the act of representation *reflects* existing societal preferences and interests.[52] Looking at Congress and the president from the perspective of unitary democracy makes us aware of a dynamic in American policy making that we might not otherwise see.

NOTES

1. "The Candidates and the Borders," *New York Times,* April 28, 1983, A22.
2. Thomas Jefferson, "First Inaugural Address," in James D. Richardson, *A Compilation of the Messages and Papers of the Presidents* (New York: Bureau of National Literature, 1897), 1: 312; Wilson and Kennedy quoted in Thomas E. Cronin, *The State of the Presidency* (Boston: Little, Brown, 1980), 75.
3. Unnamed members, quoted in Lewis Anthony Dexter, *The Sociology and Politics of Congress* (New York: Rand McNally, 1969), 154.
4. Unnamed representative, quoted in Richard F. Fenno, Jr., *Congressmen in Committees* (Boston: Little, Brown, 1973); former Rep. Michael Myers (D Pa.), quoted in Roger H. Davidson and Walter J. Oleszek, *Congress and Its Members* (Washington, D.C.: CQ Press, 1981), 108.
5. Respectively, Grant McConnell, *The Modern Presidency* (New York: St. Martin's, 1976), 42; Richard A. Watson and Norman C. Thomas, *The Politics of the Presidency* (New York: Wiley, 1983), 246-247; and James L. Sundquist, *The Decline and Resurgence of Congress* (Washington, D.C.: Brookings Institution, 1981), 451. See also Charles O. Jones, "Presidential Negotiation with Congress," in *Both Ends of the Avenue: The Presidency, the Executive Branch, and Congress in the 1980s,* ed. Anthony King (Washington, D.C.: American Enterprise Institute, 1983), 96-130, and George C. Edwards III, *Presidential Influence in Congress* (San Francisco: W. H. Freeman, 1980), 128-134.
6. Edwin S. Corwin, *The President: Office and Powers* (New York: New York University Press, 1957), 171.
7. Cf. Edwards, *Presidential Influence,* 35-48; *The Presidency and the Political System,* ed. Michael Nelson (Washington, D.C.: CQ Press, 1984), 364-367; and Davidson and Oleszek, *Congress and Its Members,* 301-303.
8. Bob Eckhardt and Charles L. Black, Jr., *The Tides of Power: Conversations on the American Constitution* (New Haven: Yale University Press, 1976), 49.

9. Grant McConnell, *Private Power and American Democracy* (New York: Vintage, 1966), 109.

10. Ibid., 110.

11. See Ronald C. Kahn, "Political Change in America: Highway Politics and Reactive Policymaking," in *Public Values and Private Power in American Politics*, ed. J. David Greenstone (Chicago: University of Chicago Press, 1982), 139-172, and Edwards, *Presidential Influence*, 19.

12. See Morris P. Fiorina, *Representatives, Roll Calls, and Constituencies* (Lexington, Mass.: Lexington Books, 1974), for findings that support the diversity-competitiveness hypothesis, and Jon R. Bond, "The Influence of Constituency Diversity on Electoral Competition in Voting for Congress, 1974-1978," *Legislative Studies Quarterly* 8 (May 1983): 201-217, for a more recent study and review of the literature. Bond's study uses a measure of population diversity based on residence, employment, income, race, and ethnicity. The average level of diversity for House districts in the 1970s was .37, lower than the state average of .41, leading Bond to conclude that "states are more diverse than congressional districts, but the differences do not appear to be great" (203). A study in line with the McConnell thesis presented here would be one that measured the relationship between district diversity and House members' support for the president.

13. Richard F. Fenno, Jr., *Home Style: House Members in Their Districts* (Boston: Little, Brown, 1978), 4.

14. Fenno recognized the difficulty of measuring the degree of homogeneity/heterogeneity in a district. He argued that it could not be directly inferred from demographic data but that "both the number and compatibility of significant interests within the district would seem to be involved. The greater the number of significant interests, the more likely it is that the district will be seen as heterogeneous. But, if the several significant interests were viewed as having a lowest common denominator and, therefore, as being quite compatible, the district might still be viewed as homogeneous. One indicator, therefore, might be the ease with which the congressman finds a lowest common denominator of interests for some large proportion of his geographical constituency." Ibid., 4-5.

15. Raymond A. Bauer, Ithiel de Sola Pool, and Lewis Anthony Dexter, *American Business and Public Policy* (Chicago: Aldine Atherton, 1972), 14.

16. Arthur Maass, *Congress and the Common Good* (New York: Basic Books, 1983), 74.

17. Edwards, *Presidential Influence*, 42-43.

18. Ibid., 43.

19. Donald R. Matthews and James A. Stimson, *Yeas and Nays: Normal Decision-Making in the U.S. House of Representatives* (New York: Wiley, 1975), 156-159.

20. Richard E. Neustadt, *Presidential Power* (New York: Wiley, 1980); *The Illusion of Presidential Government*, ed. Hugh Heclo and Lester M. Salamon (Boulder, Colo.: Westview, 1981); Alexander L. George, *Presidential Decisionmaking in Foreign Policy: The Effective Use of Information and Advice* (Boulder, Colo.: Westview, 1980); and *Rethinking the Presidency*, ed. Thomas E. Cronin (Boston: Little, Brown, 1982).

21. Edwards, *Presidential Influence*, 46-47.

22. Unnamed representative, quoted in Stephen E. Frantzich, *Computers in*

Congress: The Politics of Information (Beverly Hills, Calif.: Sage, 1982), 33; and unnamed senator, quoted in Norman J. Ornstein and David Rohde, "Resource Usage, Information, and Policymaking in the Senate," in *Congress and Public Policy*, ed. David C. Kozak and John D. Macartney (Homewood, Ill.: Dorsey, 1982), 309.

23. Quoted in Charles O. Jones, "Why Congress Can't Do Policy Analysis," *Policy Analysis* 64 (Spring 1976): 256.

24. Both quoted in David Burnham, "Computer Is Leaving a Wide Imprint on Congress," *New York Times*, April 13, 1984, B10. Frantzich, *Computers in Congress*, provides an extensive analysis of the impact of computers on Congress.

25. The rest of the representatives either did not answer in geographical terms or did not answer at all. Roger H. Davidson, *The Role of the Congressman* (New York: Pegasus, 1969), 122.

26. Ibid.

27. Philip Brenner, *The Limits and Possibilities of Congress* (New York: St. Martin's, 1983), 169-170.

28. See, for example, David R. Mayhew, *Congress: The Electoral Connection* (New Haven: Yale University Press, 1974), and Morris P. Fiorina, *Congress: Keystone of the Washington Establishment* (New Haven: Yale University Press, 1977). Fenno's observation (*Home Style*, 31) is to the point: "For most members of Congress, most of the time, this electoral goal is primary. It is the prerequisite for a congressional career and, hence, for the pursuit of other member goals."

29. Michael Nelson, "Evaluating the Presidency," in Nelson, *Presidency*, 18.

30. Ibid.

31. Thomas E. Cavanagh, "Role Orientations of House Members: The Process of Representation" (Paper delivered at the annual meeting of the American Political Science Association, Washington, D.C., 1979), 2, cited in Sundquist, *Decline and Resurgence*, 450.

32. R. Douglas Arnold, "The Local Roots of Domestic Policy," in *The New Congress*, ed. Thomas E. Mann and Norman J. Ornstein (Washington, D.C.: American Enterprise Institute, 1981), 281 and 283-284. See also Thomas E. Mann, *Unsafe at Any Margin: Interpreting Congressional Elections* (Washington, D.C.: American Enterprise Institute, 1978), 72.

33. Hanna Fenichel Pitkin, *The Concept of Representation* (Berkeley: University of California Press, 1967), 215 and 218. V. O. Key's observation is worth repeating: "Most of the time the elegant prose spilled over the question of whether the legislator should be a man and vote his mature convictions in the national interest or be a mouse and bow abjectly to the parochial demands of his constituents is irrelevant to the realities." *Public Opinion and American Democracy* (New York: Knopf, 1961), 482.

34. Joseph M. Bessette, "Is Congress a Deliberative Body?" in *The United States Congress: Proceedings of the Thomas P. O'Neill, Jr., Symposium*, ed. Dennis Hale (Chestnut Hill, Mass.: Boston College, 1982), 5.

35. Joseph M. Bessette, "Deliberative Democracy: The Majority Principle in Republican Government," in *How Democratic Is the Constitution?* (Washington, D.C.: American Enterprise Institute, 1981), 109-110.

36. Mann, *Unsafe at Any Margin*, 1.

37. Reviews of the political science literature on elections, including studies of the incumbency factor and presidential coattails, may be found in Barbara Hinckley, *Congressional Elections* (Washington, D.C.: CQ Press, 1981); Gary C. Jacobson, *The Politics of Congressional Elections* (Boston: Little, Brown, 1983); and Edwards, *Presidential Influence*, 70-78.

38. A review of legislative election studies structured in terms of the collective choice, competitive change, and voter preference models may be found in Lyn Ragsdale, "Responsiveness and Legislative Elections: Toward a Comparative Study," *Legislative Studies Quarterly* 8 (August 1983): 339-378.

39. Jacobson, *Politics of Congressional Elections*, 156. For a more extensive discussion of the indirect impact of national forces on congressional elections, see Gary C. Jacobson and Samuel Kernell, *Strategy and Choice in Congressional Elections* (New Haven: Yale University Press, 1981).

40. Hugh Heclo and Rudolph G. Penner, "Fiscal and Political Strategy in the Reagan Administration," in *The Reagan Presidency*, ed. Fred I. Greenstein (Baltimore: The Johns Hopkins University Press, 1983), 45.

41. Rep. Bruce A. Morrison, D-Conn., quoted in Steven V. Roberts, "Democratic Freshmen Hope to Make the Deficit Issue Pay Off," *New York Times*, November 13, 1983, E5.

42. Louis Fisher, *The Constitution between Friends* (New York: St. Martin's, 1978), 83.

43. Bessette, "Deliberative Democracy," 110.

44. Harold H. Bruff and Ernest Gellhorn, "Congressional Control of Administrative Regulation: A Study of Legislative Vetoes," *Harvard Law Review* 90 (May 1977): 1369-1440. For the text of the majority and dissenting opinions in *Immigration and Naturalization Service v. Chadha*, see *Congressional Quarterly Weekly Report*, June 25, 1983, 1314-1315.

45. Allen Schick, *Reconciliation and the Congressional Budget Process* (Washington, D.C.: American Enterprise Institute, 1981), 38.

46. Recent analyses can be found in Hale, *U.S. Congress*, part 4, and *Making Economic Policy in Congress*, ed. Allen Schick (Washington, D.C.: American Enterprise Institute, 1983).

47. Fred I. Greenstein, "The Need for an Early Appraisal of the Reagan Presidency," in Greenstein, *Reagan Presidency*, 4; Senator Simpson quoted in Nadine Cohodas, "O'Neill Pulls Immigration Reform Measure," *Congressional Quarterly Weekly Report*, October 8, 1983, 2088; and Lawrence O'Brien, *No Final Victories* (New York: Ballantine, 1974), 249.

48. Samuel P. Huntington, *American Politics: The Promise of Disharmony* (Cambridge: Harvard University Press, 1981), 14.

49. Alan Wolfe, "Presidential Power and the Crisis of Modernization," in Cronin, *Rethinking the Presidency*, 139-152.

50. Brenner, *Limits and Possibilities*, 188-192.

51. Fenno, *Home Style*, 246; Pitkin, *Concept of Representation*, 218; and Brenner, *Limits and Possibilities*, 180.

52. For a discussion of "state interests" that raises similar points, see Eric A. Nordlinger, *On the Autonomy of the Democratic State* (Cambridge: Harvard University Press, 1981), 31-38.

Congressional Committees 4

Because of the complexity and scope of American government, Congress relies heavily on committees to get its work done. Committees function by publicizing issues; gathering information; seeking out and trying to accommodate a range of interests; drafting, refining, and modifying legislative proposals and mobilizing political forces to obtain their enactment; and overseeing their implementation and results.[1] In the 98th Congress (1983-1984), the House had 22 and the Senate 16 standing committees. The opportunities to achieve legislators' major objectives—to enact good public policy, win reelection, and exert influence within their legislative chamber—vary among these committees, and members seek committee assignments that they believe will most closely match their own priorities.[2] Committees also differ in the extent to which unitary and adversary democracy characterize their processes and their ends, and these characteristics change over time, sometimes as a result of reforms enacted by the legislative chamber.

On the basis of the responses of members or knowledgeable staff aides to the question, "What committees did you want to serve on (after you were first elected to your chamber?)," and the reasons given for their choices, Smith and Deering classified committees as *prestige, policy,* or *constituency-oriented*, according to whether the respondents mentioned influence within the chamber, enactment of specific policies, or electoral concerns most frequently. The committees in the House were classified as follows:

Prestige	Appropriations
	Budget
	Rules
	Ways and Means
Policy	Banking, Finance and Urban Affairs
	Foreign Affairs
	Energy and Commerce
	Judiciary
	Government Operations
Constituency	Agriculture
	Armed Services
	Interior and Insular Affairs
	Merchant Marine and Fisheries
	Public Works and Transportation
	Science and Technology
	Small Business
	Veterans' Affairs

One committee, Education and Labor, was classified as both a policy and a constituency-oriented committee.[3]

Constituency Committees

Committees categorized as "constituency-oriented" tend to place a premium on achieving consensus or at least broad agreement as they develop their legislative proposals. In these committees, members follow norms of reciprocity, deference, and mutual noninterference.[4] For example, on the House Agriculture Committee there are members representing cotton, tobacco, wheat, cattle, and dairy-product interests. They divide into subcommittees dealing with those commodities and often support one another by approving omnibus bills that give price supports to each other's commodities. The Armed Services Committee follows similar norms in its efforts to protect military installations in committee members' districts. Interior's jurisdiction over public lands, mining, and water development attracts members from western states, who cooperate in passing programs that serve their constituents. Public Works authorizes funds for public buildings, highways, airports, and river and harbor projects through a process of mutual support. In each of these cases, committee members attempt to represent clearly delineated district interests.

Smith and Deering found that the full committees of the constituency type generally accept the recommendations of their subcommittees. This occurs because the interests of committee members have already been incorporated into subcommittee proposals.[5] Reciprocity between subcommittees is often evident in the full committee's consideration of subcommittee proposals. Norms of specialization and logrolling (supporting each other's proposals) are stronger on these committees than on policy committees, as is the expectation that the committee chair will support efforts at reaching consensus.[6]

Constituency committees also have policy interests that are not so directly related to members' districts. Examples include environmental and nuclear energy issues for Interior, food stamps for Agriculture, transportation issues for Public Works, energy and technology issues for Science and Technology, and, more recently, arms-control and weapons issues on Armed Services. Such issues have been sources of conflict on these committees, and the committees have made interesting adjustments to deal with them. Interior and Public Works combined subcommittees that had had a parochial focus and created new ones, such as the Energy and Environment Subcommittee, that would concentrate on issues of interest to their more policy-oriented members. The combined subcommittees continued to operate seeking consensus, but it was more difficult for the newly created ones to do so. Agriculture, in its effort to further consensus, put together a rural-urban coalition by regularly joining the food-stamp program and major farm legislation in one bill.[7] These changes show committees with a preference for operating by consensus trying to deal with the more conflictful parts of their jurisdictions.

Some constituency committees appear to be unitary subsystems in Congress as they deal with certain matters. They act as if they shared a common interest and sought to serve that interest, whether it be subsidizing agriculture, protecting military installations, authorizing dams, building highways, or supporting veterans or small business. They go out of their way to satisfy the interests of different groups in their committees, and because committee members are satisfied, they are more tolerant of unequal formal power in the committee and less interested in equal participation.[8] In these committees, the goal is to reach agreements that are supported by more than a bare majority of members; the members thus try to facilitate not only their own district's interests, but also those of their colleagues'. Toward that end, they tend to avoid the issues that divide them—such as nuclear power, weapons systems, and the environment—and stress those that unite them. In this way, they serve their own interests and also create a broad coalition of support in committee, which increases the likelihood of success on the floor.[9]

We can see the unitary side of a constituency committee at work in the response of the House Agriculture Committee to the budget cuts proposed in 1981.[10] These cuts threatened years of mutual accommodation in the committee. In fact, the director of the Office of Management and Budget, David A. Stockman, sought to reduce total farm subsidies by breaking up the agricultural coalition. His strategy was first to get support for cuts in dairy subsidies, with the expectation that dairy-interest representatives would then cease backing subsidies for other commodities, leading to a breakdown in the system of reciprocity. As Rep. Dawson Mathis, D-Ga., put it, "The theory is still valid that no commodity can stand alone." A soybean lobbyist described the situation this way: "It used to be that everybody could get their piece of the pie, and if the pie was too small, [Congress] could just make it bigger," but in that year, he said, "there's not enough to go around." Stockman's strategy seemed to be working at first. Members scrambled to save their own commodities and were less supportive of committee colleagues.

After some months, however, committee members and commodity groups realized their vulnerability resulting from these conflicts and divisions, and they resumed their support for each other's interests. When the omnibus farm bill came to the House floor in October 1981, peanut, grain, cotton, and rice supporters worked the floor for dairy interests. A food-stamp coalition leader, who had the pledge of commodity members for limitations on cuts in food stamps, said he would back all commodity supports. As a consequence, certain proposed cuts in subsidies were defeated on the floor.

To say that constituency committees sometimes act as unitary subsystems is not to suggest that they are always unitary (or that policy committees are always adversary). Every committee, regardless of type, has both unitary and adversary aspects, but committee types differ in their tendencies or their emphasis on one form of democracy or the other. From an adversary perspective, constituency committees can be said to protect individual and district interests. Sometimes those interests are largely confined to particular districts (agriculture subsidies and irrigation projects); at other times they result in a fairly universal distribution of benefits (highway construction and support for small business and veterans). Some equality of power is also achieved by these committees, since most agricultural products are subsidized, military installations are supported, and regions needing irrigation get it. Because constituency committees are usually supported on the floor when they show broad agreement on proposals, certain interests that are a minority in the nation as a whole, such as those in agriculture, are able to achieve their policy goals. This power of numerical minorities in a legislature that makes decisions by majority rule is an important part of the American political system, increasing its workability and legitimacy.[11]

Constituency committees tend not to be representative of Congress or the country in their makeup. For example, the Agriculture committees in both chambers are disproportionately southern and midwestern, and there is an overrepresentation of westerners on the Interior committees.[12] This occurs because membership on constituency committees (though not only on them) is largely self-recruited; that is, members request assignment to these committees and are often granted their choices.[13] Most seek assignment to these committees in order to deliver benefits to particular groups and localities, and they are relatively unconcerned with the question of who will pay for those benefits.

Constituency committees could be made more responsive to broader, less parochial perspectives when their bills came to the chamber floors, where interests not protected by these committees— taxpayers, consumers, and those who do not receive the particular subsidies—would be better represented. However, if committees have found that they can get floor support for legislation by achieving broad agreement in committee, they will not be concerned about that possibility, especially if it is not particularly difficult to achieve wide agreement. Committees can also gain floor support by distributing benefits among many states and districts. Insofar as legislators are interested in providing distributive benefits to their constituencies more than they are in the costs of such provisions, committees can win support for legislation by shaping their proposals accordingly. This tactic is particularly characteristic of committees like Public Works, Armed Services, Small Business, and Veterans' Affairs. Moreover, members are sometimes willing to support benefits for particular groups in order to accommodate their colleagues, as long as the programs in question are not seen as having significant adverse effects on their own district or state. Finally, insofar as members believe that politicians succeed in elections and in the chamber by saying "yes" more than "no," they are apt to support constituency-committee proposals on the floor; they hope that this will bring reciprocal support from colleagues on other matters of greater interest to them.

All of this limits floor constraints on constituency committees, even when committee membership is unrepresentative of Congress as a whole and those committees serve narrow ends. The parochialism of constituency committees may not be overcome by members on the floor, if they fail to adopt a broader perspective in evaluating legislation from those committees. Insofar as the chambers are supportive of constituency committees, the chambers' formal powers of control over committee behavior, through jurisdiction realignment, multiple referral, minority staffing, constraints on the conduct of hearings, and short-term authorizations and appropriations, are not likely to be used to sharply limit these committees.[14]

In sum, constituency committees operate as unitary democracies seeking consensus. However, they employ unitary processes primarily for adversary ends, to protect the interests of individuals and groups in committee members' districts. Since, as is the case here, a unitary process can serve adversary ends, one must assess the democratic significance of both the process and the substance of congressional action. From an adversary point of view, certain interests are not well represented by constituency committees; in the unitary perspective, they pay too little attention to serving broad national interests. Even granting that the particular interests represented by constituency committees are part of the nation and deserve consideration as part of the national interest, there are wider interests that also need to be considered.

Policy Committees

Policy committees, those whose members are more likely to cite policy reasons for wanting to be on them, deal with issues that are often more salient nationally and more conflictful than the issues before constituency committees. Their jurisdictions are more fragmented and involve a greater variety of policies.[15] For example, the House Energy and Commerce Committee is concerned with energy, air pollution, consumer protection, health, and trade—issues that are highly controversial and frequently objects of attention in the national media.

The consequences of these differences between policy and constituency committees are substantial. The norms of reciprocity, deference, and noninterference between committee members are weaker in policy committees. Subcommittee recommendations are more likely to be challenged in the full committee, and committee proposals are more likely to be challenged on the chamber floor. Because members are attracted to these committees for policy reasons, they often have their own policy agendas and a desire to participate in a wide variety of committee concerns. Consequently, the House reforms of the 1970s, which opened up subcommittee participation, resulted in further intensification of subcommittee activity on these committees.[16]

The fact that members wish to be on particular committees in order to make good public policy does not mean that they will ignore individual and district interests—and policy committees do also deal with issues of interest to particular districts. For example, a number of House members from the northeast joined the Commerce Committee in the late 1970s to protect constituents in that energy-consuming area from substantial increases in the cost of energy. Because policy committees affect substantial economic interests, members can elicit campaign contributions and other resources from those they support.[17] Members can therefore work to achieve particular policies and serve their goal of reelection even when those policies are of marginal interest to most of their constituents.

While we cannot be certain in any given case that a policy-committee member is seeking to serve the national interest rather than a district or some other interest, the fact that so many issues handled by these committees are not salient to most members' constituents suggests that serving interests beyond those of the district may well be part of members' motivation for serving on these committees. That these House policy committees are more popular than constituency committees indicates the importance of policy considerations in Congress.[18]

The desire to serve more than district interests suggests unitary considerations, but some of the behavior of the policy committees is not consistent with the unitary model. Unlike some constituency committees, policy committees do not ordinarily make decisions by consensus or even by large majorities, nor do their subcommittees.[19] This does not mean that members are not striving to achieve common interests. Rather, it reflects sharp conflict over the issues, conflict that cannot be reconciled through a consensual process. Members of these committees do not expect to achieve broad agreement; in fact, appeals made by opposing sides of the subcommittees at the committee and floor stages indicate the belief that the issue will be settled instead by a keenly contested vote. When individuals have irreconcilable conflicts about the public interest, they are in a situation of adversary democracy. That these committees usually operate as adversary democracies can be seen in the fact that members strive vigorously for equal power and participation.[20] Policy committees have seen a greater increase in subcommittee activity than have constituency committees. They have also made greater use of the "Subcommittee Bill of Rights," enacted in 1973, which took the power to control subcommittee staff, bill referral, and subcommittee appointments away from the committee chair and gave it to the full committee.[21]

What can be said about these policy committees from an adversary point of view? Because they have large and fragmented jurisdictions, it is harder for particular interests to dominate them. For example, the Commerce Committee is of great interest to the oil, communications, transportation, and automobile industries, and also to environmentalists and the consumer movement, and all of these interests want to have sympathetic members on the committee. Consequently, no single industry or interest dominates that body. While the Commerce Committee could, like Agriculture, divide into subcommittees representing particular industries or causes which would then support each other's recommendations in the full committee, this does not happen; rather, conflict occurs quite often in full committee. Because no one interest or set of interests does dominate, influence over policy is more equal. This greater competitiveness can also limit committee parochialism, which is a desirable outcome from a unitary perspective.

What most promotes adversary democracy in policy committees is the conflict in its agenda and its legislative environment, so often lacking in constituency committees. However, even though policy committees exhibit qualities of adversary democracy, they do not necessarily achieve two other adversary standards: equality of power, and outcomes proportional to numbers. While multiple interests are brought into conflict on these committees, not all interests are represented equally. Intense, organized, and resourceful interests have advantages here as in other congressional domains. But, in contrast with what happens in constituency committees, the salience of the issues that policy committees deal with makes it more likely that broader interests will come into play.

Prestige Committees

The defining characteristic of prestige committees is that the chief motivation for joining them is to exert influence within the chamber. These are enormously important committees. Ways and Means has broad jurisdiction, most importantly over tax policy, but also over international trade, social security, Medicare, public assistance, and unemployment compensation. Appropriations deals with program funding, an obviously critical area, and Budget with general spending levels, taxation levels, and the deficit. Each of these committees is in a position to take up more than district concerns. Each can focus on important national questions that involve difficult choices about raising taxes, limiting spending, or imposing fiscal constraints on Congress. Mayhew calls the House Ways and Means, Appropriations, and Rules committees "control committees," because they are in a position to control some of the excesses of Congress, such as high levels of spending, a reluctance to raise sufficient revenues to support that spending, and an overly local and clientele-oriented focus in dealing with fiscal matters.[22]

Prestige committees have tended toward unitary democracy. This has been evident in the ways in which they have historically tried to limit parochialism. Ways and Means, for example, has used a closed rule on tax and trade matters, which limits special-interest amendments on the floor; and it was once a custom for the Appropriations chair to place members on subcommittees in which their district had no distinctive interest.[23]

Since the 1960s, however, Appropriations and Ways and Means seem to have moved away from their unitary emphasis. For example, Appropriations has shown less of a tendency to reduce executive spending requests and an increased tendency to appropriate funds for district- and clientele-oriented projects and programs.[24] This took place during a period when the full House tried to get around committee, presidential, and even congressional spending limits by passing entitlements and other permanent appropriations that would be mandated by law and thus not require Appropriations Committee approval. The shift in Appropriations Committee behavior was hastened by making committee markups public, decreasing committee members' willingness to reject spending requests. The chair's power to name subcommittees and their leaders was also taken away by the reforms mentioned earlier. Consequently, the previous practice of placing members on subcommittees in such a way as to minimize constituency pressures and free them to cut spending came to an end. Members now choose their subcommittees in order to be able to support the interests they favor, and the full committee, operating on the basis of reciprocity, tends to support the recommendations of its subcommittees. In short, the behavior of the Appropriations Committee has become more like that of a constituency committee.

Appropriations subcommittee chairs, unlike those of any other committee, are now subject to approval by the full Democratic caucus and are thus sensitive to the wishes of representatives who are not committee members. Clearly, the ability of the committee to reflect national or unitary considerations, and to balance some of the parochial, particularistic, and clientele-oriented tendencies of the House, has been reduced over the last 15 years. The more liberal funding of most programs that has resulted might be considered by some to be in furtherance of the national interest, despite the lack of selectivity involved, but an important source of a unitary perspective has been lost, at least for the time being.

Similar changes took place in the House Ways and Means Committee. Previously, as already noted, Ways and Means operated much of the time under a closed rule, especially in tax legislation. This precluded amendments from the floor and required members to vote on the committee's bills as all-or-nothing propositions. It justified this rule on the ground that tax bills were too complex and important for uninformed members to tamper with on the floor. This limited parochialism and clientelism, at least on the floor. The committee also marked up its bills in closed session most of the time, again limiting the influence of interest groups. But the Democratic caucus then passed rules making it easier to offer amendments to committee bills from the floor, and the reforms of the 1970s opened up committee markups. Consequently, the Ways and Means Committee has become more partisan and divided.[25] Its members are less insulated from attempts by outside groups and nonmembers of the committee to influence legislation than they had been before. The restrictions on its power were reinforced by another reform that deprived its Democratic members of their role as that party's Committee on Committees, which had nominated party colleagues to committees. Ways and Means became more permeable to outside influence and less able to resist parochial and clientele influence.[26]

The House itself was basically in an adversary mode on both appropriations and tax issues during this period, and as a result these two committees moved in the same direction. But the opening up of these committees also reflected a loss of trust in them. House members apparently no longer felt confident the committees were doing what members wanted. Changes in the committees themselves—for example, open markups of bills—strengthened the legislator-constituency focus of committee members and reduced the dominance of the legislator-legislator focus within committee that is associated with unitary democracy.[27] Growing emphasis on more equal power and participation in each committee and loss of a consensual approach in Ways and Means also indicate a move toward more adversary patterns of behavior. Changes in emphasis and subcommittee reciprocity in the Appropriations Committee might suggest it adopted a unitary approach within committee similar to that of constituency committees. In fact, one could argue that it has become a constituency committee and has lost some of its focus on broader concerns such as limiting government spending.

On the other hand, these changes facilitated the representation of individual and district interests. Whether the major evaluative standards of adversary democracy—equal protection of interests and outcomes proportional to numbers—have been met or even approximated by these changes is another question. More equal power and participation by committee members and more opportunity for nonmembers of the committee to influence their deliberations may contribute to a more equal protection of interests, but it is not the same as nor does it assure such equal protection. As long as organized, intense interests and well-financed groups are more likely to be heard in these committees, the standard of equal protection will not be met. Those interests are more likely to be represented in the present, more permeable, Ways and Means Committee than they were earlier. The same is not necessarily true, however, for unorganized, resource-poor, and uninformed or unaware individuals and groups. The potential for inequality in the protection of interests certainly exists.

Senate Committees

Senate committees generally are more permeable to nonmembers than are House committees.[28] This is partly due to the Senate's smaller size and the resultant stronger personal relationships among members. Senators also have links to more committees than representatives do, because of multiple assignments. The average senator had 11.6 committee and subcommittee assignments in the 98th Congress, while the average representative served on 5.8 committees and subcommittees.[29] Furthermore, floor deliberation is more important in the Senate. It is more acceptable there for a nonmember to propose important amendments to committee legislation. Underlying these conditions is the fact that states are more heterogeneous than are House districts, which leads senators to attempt to influence more issues than representatives typically do.

Perhaps because committees are less important in the Senate, senators mention influence in the chamber as a reason for seeking assignment to particular committees much less frequently than representatives. Senators are more likely than representatives to mention constituency-oriented goals.[30] This probably reflects both the greater heterogeneity of states and the greater competitiveness of Senate seats.

Permeable Senate committees serve senators' constituency-oriented needs better than less permeable House committees would. Because Senate committees are less autonomous than their House counterparts, and because senators' responsibilities are spread over more areas, there has been less movement in the direction of increased subcommittee autonomy in the Senate. Subcommittee autonomy is of less value if committee autonomy is limited.[31]

The greater permeability of Senate committees and more pervasive constituency orientation of senators can be seen in comparisons of parallel committees in the two chambers. Most striking is a comparison of four of the most important committees in both chambers, the tax and appropriations committees. In the 1960s, the Senate Appropriations Committee was much less likely to reduce the executive budget than was its House counterpart, and it even tended to restore spending cuts made in the House. Similarly, the Senate Finance Committee was much more likely to grant tax benefits than was the House Ways and Means Committee.[32] The Senate committees were acting as "appeals courts" following initial House consideration. However, as the House Appropriations and Ways and Means committees became more permeable in the 1970s, differences between the two chambers with respect to these committees declined.

The Senate thus appears to be more adversary than the House. The work of its committees is more affected by efforts on the part of nonmembers to protect constituency interests. Its tax and spending committees have lacked the unitary concerns of their House counterparts, although those differences are narrowing. Nevertheless, the Senate is not necessarily less unitary in orientation. Nonmembers of a committee may be trying to serve a national rather than a limited constituency interest in attempting to influence committee actions. Senators themselves seem to draw a less sharp distinction between policy and constituency-oriented motivation than representatives do, perhaps because in taking policy stands, senators gain publicity and reelection benefits not so readily available to representatives.[33] That many senators are potential presidential candidates and hence are able to get national publicity more easily than representatives also leads them to be concerned with policies affecting constituencies beyond their states. That senators have larger staffs, are able to influence a wider range of issues, have longer terms, and belong to a smaller body all probably affect their willingness to get involved in issues of more than local importance. All this can lead to development of unitary perspectives on the part of senators. On the other hand, greater electoral competition and constituency heterogeneity can push senators in adversary directions. In the end, each member of Congress finds his or her own balance in pursuing adversary and unitary goals. Opportunities in the Senate, however, permit members of that chamber to be both more adversary and more unitary than representatives.

Sources of Adversary and Unitary Modes in Committees

The committees of the two chambers not only make different kinds of contributions to unitary and adversary goals, but they also have different ways of making policy. Some operate in a relatively adversarial, conflictful mode and others in a more unitary, consensual one. What causes these different patterns of policy making?[34]

Constituency committees operate in an environment consisting of well-defined, relatively homogeneous constituencies, which the committees can serve with a consensual approach. Policy committees' environments and agendas are more prone to conflict and those conflicts are more salient; these committees' jurisdictions are more fragmented and their constituents more diverse. When conflicts do arise in constituency committees, they are usually of the positive-sum kind, in which gains by one subgroup are not incompatible with gains by other subgroups. These committees also deal primarily with distributive policies, those that determine the distribution of government benefits, and agreement and consensus are easier to achieve in these areas. In contrast, policy committees frequently deal with zero-sum or constant-sum conflicts, in which one group's gain is seen as another's loss, and they deal primarily with regulatory rather than distributive policies.[35]

Prestige committees have differed across chambers and, in the House at least, they have changed over time. Appropriations and tax committees have been more distributive in approach in the Senate than in the House, although those differences became less clear-cut in the 1970s. As noted above, the House Ways and Means Committee has become more conflictful. The differences and changes in these committees suggest that they are affected by members' purposes and identifications, and not only by committee jurisdictions and agendas.[36]

The committee reforms of the 1970s, especially in the House, also have implications for congressional democracy. A most important set of reforms was that limiting the power of House committee chairs. Prior to these reforms, committee chairs had the power to create subcommittees, assign members to them, determine their jurisdiction, staff, and budget, and refer bills to them. House rules now require committees to specify the jurisdictions of subcommittees. Committee members are permitted to select subcommittees to serve on in order of committee seniority, and no member can choose a second subcommittee assignment until every member has one. Committee chairs are required to refer bills to appropriate subcommittees. Subcommittee staffs and budgets are determined by the full committees. Committee members from the majority party bid in order of committee seniority for subcommittee chairs and must receive a majority of committee members' votes to gain those positions.[37] These changes have promoted adversary democracy in Congress by making the members of committees more nearly equal.

The new rule that committee chairs and House Appropriations subcommittee chairs must be approved by the party caucus before the start of each Congress also strengthens adversary democracy, because it creates an additional incentive for these chairs to be responsive to the chamber and their committees. Transferring power over Democratic committee assignments in the House from the Democrats on the Ways and Means Committee to the Democratic Steering and Policy Committee (which consists of party leaders and their appointees, selected committee chairs, and additional members elected by region) made control over committee appointments more democratic. While these reforms increased majority-party control, in both chamber and committee, the minority party benefited from other changes, such as one giving the minority one-third of the committee staff in the House and increasing its share of committee staff in the Senate.

Another important reform in both chambers has been the requirement that all committee meetings, including bill markups, be open to the public (unless the committee publicly votes to close a meeting on a given day). This change strengthened the legislator-constituency focus and weakened the legislator-legislator focus. In 1980, a four-member task force of the Select Committee on Committees reported that the change had inhibited the range of discussion and the willingness of members to explore controversial issues in committee meetings. The task force also said the rule made it more difficult for members to change their positions, subjected legislators to undue pressure from lobbyists and special-interest representatives, and inhibited the compromises and discussions that are an essential part of House-Senate conference committee meetings.[38] While members can still meet informally to carry on the tasks of deliberation and bargaining, such meetings are not always convenient. Thus, the rule may well have had the effect of inhibiting some important aspects of unitary democracy. That illustrates how a concern with *one* form of democracy, in this case adversary, can lead to reforms that weaken the other form. This so-called "sunshine" rule also probably strengthened the representation of those groups with incentives and resources to take greatest advantage of the new opportunities.

Because Senate committees are more permeable and exercise less influence over policy than do House committees, senators have not carried out analogous reforms. For example, neither Senate nor party caucus rules limit chairs' control over subcommittee jurisdictions, majority committee staff, or subcommittee bill referral and discharge.[39] Because the Senate is smaller and more informal, it did not feel the same need to increase member equality through reforms; senators, after all, were relatively equal compared to House members to start with. This interpretation is consistent with the argument that the Senate better facilitated adversary democracy than did the prereform House. It is also true, however, that the Senate has attempted to make members more nearly equal by giving junior and minority members additional staff assistance.

The reforms in the House have had greater effect on policy and prestige committees than on constituency committees. For example, the largest growth in subcommittee activity has occurred in policy committees.[40] Because these committees operate more like adversary democracies, they place a greater premium on equalizing power. The more unitary constituency committees have had less need to seek more equal power.

Conclusion

Members of Congress must decide the relative emphasis they will give to local and national considerations, particular and general perspectives, adversary and unitary approaches, and electoral and policy consequences. These considerations are not necessarily mutually exclusive; local considerations can be part of a concern for the common interest, and electoral concerns can motivate a policy focus. Nevertheless, members must make choices among alternatives, whether they do so deliberately or not. It is in the various congressional committees that these choices begin to play themselves out. Constituency committees pursue adversary goals, such as the protection of particular interests, though often through unitary means. Tensions arise between adversary and unitary considerations in some important prestige committees, and the resolution of that tension changes over time. Some policy areas lend themselves to unitary approaches and others to adversary ones, and that, too, changes over time.

Congressional committees rarely are pure types. Members of constituency committees have policy concerns, and those on policy committees are motivated by district interests. Nevertheless, the committees do have different tendencies. One can see adversary or unitary strains in particular committees at certain times and situations. Because committees can utilize a unitary process for adversary purposes, patterns of member interaction or process must be distinguished from policy context, for each may be adversary or unitary. Because adversary and unitary democracy have standards of evaluation, we can assess what Congress does well and less well as it operates in both modes. In congressional committees, the standards of one type of democracy should not be used to the exclusion of the other, for both are required, nor should the standards of one type be used to evaluate a process or context for which the other is more appropriate.[41] Each of the two modes of democracy provides a set of important and distinct standards for evaluating the committees of Congress.

NOTES

1. David Price, "Congressional Committees in the Policy Process," in *Congress Reconsidered*, 2nd ed., ed. Lawrence C. Dodd and Bruce I. Oppenheimer (Washington, D.C.: CQ Press, 1981), 159.
2. Richard F. Fenno, Jr., *Congressmen in Committees* (Boston: Little, Brown, 1973), 1-2.
3. Steven S. Smith and Christopher Deering, *Committees in Congress* (Washington: CQ Press, 1984), 90. See also David J. Vogler, *The Politics of Congress*, 4th ed. (Boston: Allyn & Bacon, 1983), 156ff. This typology does not mean that members on constituency committees have no policy motivations or that those on policy committees have no constituency concerns. Rather, the typology suggests different emphases across committee types. Smith and Deering classified four House committees as "undesired": District of Columbia, House Administration, Post Office and Civil Service, and Standards of Official Conduct. Their classification of Senate committees is somewhat different and will be discussed later in the chapter.
4. Smith and Deering, *Committees*, 177-178 and 182.
5. For a more complete account, see ibid., 143.
6. Ibid., 182. Mutual support and deference, while frequent, are not automatic on constituency committees. For example, after the 1981 budget resolution had put a ceiling on the total dollars available for agricultural support, conflicts over peanuts, tobacco, and sugar broke out, reflecting some division

in the farm bloc. See *Congressional Quarterly Weekly Report*, August 27, 1983, 1713. In present terms, members moved from a unitary to an adversary situation because of the limits placed on total agricultural expenditures. After some initial difficulty over peanut and sugar subsidies, the farm-food stamp coalition was reestablished in the House in an effort to limit program cuts. *1981 Congressional Quarterly Almanac* (Washington, D.C.: Congressional Quarterly Inc., 1981), 544.

7. Smith and Deering, *Committees*, 184.

8. Ibid., 183. One study has suggested that not all constituency committees are unitary subsystems; see Glenn R. Parker and Suzanne L. Parker, "The Size of Successful Coalitions in Congressional Committee Decision Making" (Paper delivered at the annual meeting of the American Political Science Association, Chicago, September 1983). For example, the Interior Committee does not appear to be unitary on certain issues, on which western, Republican, pro-development members are opposed by non-western, Democratic, pro-environmental members. However, Parker and Parker made their assessments of conflict and consensus on the basis of roll-call votes in the committees. But when unity prevails, committees often take voice rather than roll-call votes, so the cleavages that Parker and Parker describe may not fully reveal the degree of unity in a committee. The same comment applies to the work of Joseph K. Unekis and Leroy N. Rieselbach, *Congressional Committee Politics* (New York: Praeger, 1984). Both works show changes in conflict and consensus patterns within individual committees over time.

9. Unekis and Rieselbach, *Congressional Committee Politics*, 56-60, found that committee unity is positively correlated with floor success.

10. This material is based on *1981 Congressional Quarterly Almanac*, 535-548, and Elizabeth Wehr, "Veto, Farm Tensions Cloud Omnibus Bills," *Congressional Quarterly Weekly Report*, July 11, 1981, 1259-1260.

11. Jane J. Mansbridge, "Living with Conflict: Representation in the Theory of Adversary Democracy," *Ethics* 99 (April 1981): 471-472, discusses the problem created when members of a permanent minority have much less than equal weight in a legislature that makes decisions by majority rule. They receive none of the distributed noncollective benefits if the majority chooses not to share these with them; that is, outcomes are not distributed proportionally to numbers.

12. Smith and Deering, *Committees*, 116.

13. Kenneth Shepsle, *The Giant Jigsaw Puzzle: Democratic Committee Assignments in the Modern House* (Chicago: University of Chicago Press, 1978). Since the constituency committees are generally low in attractiveness (except for Armed Services and Interior, which ranked fifth and seventh of 20 committees in the 93rd through the 97th Congresses), members are more likely to be successful in their requests to serve on these committees: see Bruce A. Ray, "Committee Attractiveness in the U.S. House, 1963-1981," *American Journal of Political Science* 26 (August 1982): 610. Three-fourths of House Democrats applying for constituency committees were successful in the 95th through 97th Congresses; the comparable success rate for policy and prestige committees was 60 percent and less than 50 percent, respectively; Smith and Deering, *Committees*, 242.

14. These methods of chamber control of committees are discussed in Arthur

Maass, *Congress and the Common Good* (New York: Basic Books, 1983), 102-103. As will be pointed out later, the controls Maass points to are more significant in their application to policy and prestige committees than to constituency committees.

15. Smith and Deering, *Committees*, 61-71. One policy committee that has produced relatively little conflict is the House Foreign Affairs Committee; see Parker and Parker, "Successful Coalitions," 16. For some reasons why this is so, see note 35 below.

16. Smith and Deering, *Committees*, 137-140.

17. For example, in the 1981-1982 election cycle, members of the House Commerce Committee received more PAC money than any other House committee, except for Ways and Means, the House tax-writing committee. The average contribution per member from PACs was $118,000: Andy Plattner, "Scrappy House Energy Panel Provides High Pressure Arena for Wrangling over Regulation," *Congressional Quarterly Weekly Report*, March 12, 1983, 504.

18. Ray, "Committee Attractiveness," 610. Using Ray's data and his measure of committee drawing power, House policy committees had an average drawing power of .076 in the 93rd through the 97th Congresses, while constituency committees had an average drawing power of .051.

19. The exception again is Foreign Affairs; see Parker and Parker, "Successful Coalitions."

20. Jane J. Mansbridge, *Beyond Adversary Democracy* (New York: Basic Books, 1981), 30-31. Smith and Deering, *Committees*, 140, point out that equal power and participation have been less important in the Government Operations Committee, because it does relatively little legislating and more oversight.

21. Smith and Deering, *Committees*, 137-145.

22. David Mayhew, *Congress: The Electoral Connection* (New Haven: Yale University Press, 1974), 149-156. This section will deal with only the House Ways and Means and Appropriations committees. The Rules Committee will be discussed in chapter 5, because of its importance to the floor and party operations, and the Budget Committee will be discussed in chapter 8.

23. See Richard F. Fenno, Jr., *The Power of the Purse* (Boston: Little, Brown, 1966), and John F. Manley, *The Politics of Finance* (Boston: Little, Brown, 1970).

24. Smith and Deering, *Committees*, 93-94.

25. Ibid., 96-97.

26. The concept of "committee permeability" comes from Fenno, *Congressmen in Committee*, 279. In July 1983, Ways and Means again closed its markups of tax legislation (*Congressional Quarterly Weekly Report*, October 8, 1983, 2067). Whether this signals some movement back toward more unitary concerns remains to be seen. The critical role of the committee in the budget process and the difficult decisions it has to make might explain such movement.

27. It might be said that committee members have at least two general constituencies, the voters in their districts (including clientele groups) and their colleagues in the full chamber. The connections with both were strengthened. In this book, the term "constituencies" is used in the traditional way, to refer to citizens and groups who are not members of the legislative body.

28. Smith and Deering, *Committees*, 78.

29. Norman J. Ornstein et al., *Vital Statistics on Congress, 1984-1985 Edition* (Washington, D.C.: American Enterprise Institute, 1984), 111.
30. Smith and Deering, *Committees*, 111-112. In Smith and Deering's classification of Senate committees, the policy committees are Budget, Foreign Relations, Governmental Affairs, Judiciary, and Labor and Human Resources; the constituency committees are Agriculture, Nutrition, and Forestry, Appropriations, Commerce, Science, and Transportation, Energy and Natural Resources (formerly Interior), and Environment and Public Works; and Armed Services, Banking, Housing and Urban Affairs, Finance, and Small Business are mixed constituency/policy committees. Note that Senate Commerce and Appropriations are constituency committees, while Finance and Banking are mixed constituency/policy committees; the differences between the classification of these four committees and their House counterparts reflect a greater constituency orientation in the Senate. On the other hand, Senate Armed Services and Small Business are rated as mixed policy-constituency committees and Labor as a policy committee; these three show a greater policy orientation in their ratings than their House counterparts. Smith and Deering do not classify any Senate committees as prestige committees, since for none of them was chamber infuence the most frequently mentioned objective of those who sought appointment to it.
31. Smith and Deering, *Committees*, 161.
32. Fenno, *Congressmen in Committees*, 156-161.
33. Smith and Deering, *Committees*, 111.
34. The following analysis is based partly on Smith and Deering, *Committees*, 79.
35. The distinction between distributive and regulatory policies is drawn from Theodore Lowi, "American Business, Public Policy, Case Studies, and Political Theory," *World Politics* 16 (July 1964): 689-690. The Foreign Affairs and Foreign Relations committees are "exceptions" that support the present analysis. Although they are policy committees, their constituency environments have been relatively homogeneous, and foreign policy, since Vietnam and until recently, has generally not been an area of great conflict. Consequently, they have functioned in a relatively nonpartisan, unitary manner.
36. A similar point is made in Price, "Congressional Committees," 171-172.
37. A number of these matters are controlled by the majority-party caucus in the committees. Once the caucus has made its decisions on these organizational questions, it votes as a bloc in full committee and thereby determines the outcome. Subcommittee chairs on the House Appropriations Committee, unlike any other committee, are voted on by the full House Democratic Caucus.
38. Maass, *Congress and the Common Good*, 63.
39. Smith and Deering, *Committees*, 173-174.
40. Ibid., 137.
41. Mansbridge, *Beyond Adversary Democracy*, 300.

Congressional Procedures and Parties | 5

Many of the procedural elements of congressional decision making have direct and indirect effects on the legislative ability to achieve either adversary or unitary democracy. Among them are the operations of the House Rules Committee, the recording of votes on the floor, and unanimous consent agreements and the rules of cloture in the Senate. The nature of floor deliberation and debate, the role of political parties, and party leadership also affect adversary and unitary performance. Recent changes in some of these elements have altered their effects.

The House Rules Committee

In the House, important bills usually must receive a rule from the Rules Committee before they can be considered on the floor. (Notable exceptions are tax and appropriations bills and budget resolutions.) Once a bill is reported out of committee, it ordinarily goes to the Rules Committee for a rule that specifies the amount of time allotted for general debate (usually two to four hours), the division of time between the majority and minority parties (an even division in most cases), and any restrictions on amendments when general debate is over. The power that this procedure gave the Rules Committee was seen in the late 1950s, when a coalition of Republican members of the committee and southern Democrats was able to prevent action on social welfare legislation simply by refusing to report rules for the bills. As a result, the committee was enlarged in 1961 so that it could be controlled by Democrats supporting the party's program.[1] In the mid-1970s, the committee became even more of an arm of party leadership when the Speaker was given authority to nominate its Democratic members, subject to approval by the Democratic caucus. At the same time, the Democratic caucus was authorized to instruct Democratic members of the Rules Committee to allow certain amendments to come up during floor consideration. These changes generally strengthened adversary democracy in the House by facilitating majority rule and reducing the inequality of power that existed when eight members of the Rules Committee could prevent a bill from going to the floor.

Other changes in the Rules Committee, however—and even some of the same ones—have furthered unitary democracy. For example, the Speaker's power to nominate Democratic Rules Committee members and the resulting closer tie between the committee and the majority-party leadership has meant that the committee can sometimes propose rules that allow legislation to pass that otherwise would not. This can permit passage of some difficult and perhaps unpopular legislation that most members see as being in the common interest but might have trouble supporting. To illustrate, the gradual decontrol of the price of natural gas, a centerpiece of the energy legislation of the 1970s, passed the House because the conference report on energy was treated as one bill rather than five separate bills under the rule that guided floor consideration. Had the natural-gas part of the omnibus energy bill been considered separately, indications were that that part of the program would have been defeated. However, while the changes in the operations of the Rules Committee can be said to have strengthened unitary as well as adversary aspects of congressional democracy, probably the most important change has been the reduced ability of the committee to prevent a majority from acting, a change that on balance facilitates adversary democracy.

Recording of Votes

Once a bill has received a rule from the Rules Committee and come to the floor, a majority of the House must vote for the rule before general debate can begin. Following general debate, amendments are offered and debated. Until 1970, voting in the House Committee of the Whole (the House floor operating under a quorum requirement of 100 rather than 218 members and other rules to facilitate consideration of major bills), where crucial votes on amendments take place, was in the form of voice, division, or teller votes. In a voice vote, members yell out yea or nay and the presiding officer announces which side won. Members may also request a division vote, in which members stand and are counted, or a teller vote, in which members join a yea or nay line and file past vote counters or "tellers." None of these procedures produces a record of how individual members voted on any amendments. Consequently, members could vote anonymously to weaken a bill during the amending process and then be recorded for the bill in a roll-call vote at final passage. As part of the 1970 reforms, House rules were changed to permit votes of individual members to be recorded in a teller vote. Three years later, the House moved to an electronic voting system. If 25 or more members call for a record vote under this system, legislators go to one of the voting stations on the floor, insert coded identification cards, and push the appropriate button to vote. The procedure takes only 15 minutes. The time needed to complete a record vote in the House was cut in half, and the number of such votes doubled.

The fact that members are on record much more often now than before has strengthened adversary democracy by making legislators' behavior more visible to constituents. On the other hand, the interpretation of members' votes is not always easy and can be misleading, even for those more attentive to the process than the typical citizen is.[2] Representatives may vote against a measure in the form in which it is presented even though they favor the general concept. Or they may oppose particular parts of a measure but vote for it because they think on balance it merits support. They may vote on the basis of procedural considerations—for example, to oppose a closed rule—even though they favor the substance of the legislation that rule pertains to. They may oppose abortions personally but not want to amend the Constitution to ban them. In short, members can appear to stand on both sides of an issue, either as a result of careful thought or in order to obscure their position for political reasons, such as an effort to placate a divided constituency. While recorded votes facilitate citizens' ability to hold representatives accountable, these possibilities suggest caution in doing so. The inattention and ignorance of most constituents, however, mean that such caution will rarely be exercised by most citizens. Because of limited public attention, members are sometimes confronted with a choice of voting in a way they consider best but would have a hard time explaining, or voting in a way that is easier to explain even though they would prefer to be on the other side.

The increase in recorded floor votes has had important implications for adversary and unitary democracy. To quote a member who had been active in the reforms of the 1970s: "Recorded votes in the Committee of the Whole have been a mixed blessing. The bells are continually ringing. You can't get your work done. Even if you're not interested in a bill, you have to be on the floor. People are voting in greater ignorance now. The guys don't know the bill they're voting on, let alone the amendments." [3] This same member, generally regarded as a liberal, described how in the civil rights struggles of the 1960s the problem was getting members to the floor "whose press releases on the issue I had just been reading in the morning papers." At the same time, he pointed out, those who were on the floor during the 1960s were really interested in the bills that were being considered. But, as has already been noted, those really interested in a bill may have had particular and parochial concerns unrepresentative of the full membership. Thus, the advent of record votes in the Committee of the Whole allowed a more representative group to control decisions at that stage. On the other hand, it led to more votes by those lacking knowledge about and interest in the issues before them. Since members do not like to be recorded as absent, for fear it will be used against them in elections, they choose to vote on more occasions than they did prior to reform, when their absences were less visible. The House member previously quoted also said, "The doorman has become the most powerful man in the House." The reference in this perhaps somewhat exaggerated statement is to the party employee at the entrance to the floor, who gives a thumbs up or down sign, or some similar signal, to members as they come into the chamber from their party's cloakroom. Another member said: "Cue givers influence the votes more than consideration of debate on the floor. Since members have 15 minutes to get to the floor to vote, they don't have to be on the floor and so don't get the spirit of the debate and disagreements. We need to find ways to keep guys there so they will have more time to speak with members and come to conclusions, more time to stimulate their memories." However, in 1979 the practice of televising House floor proceedings began; since the telecasts are transmitted to members' offices, the effect has probably been to increase the amount of information about floor debate that is available to members and staff.

Voting Cues

The need to vote on so many matters means members cannot know everything they would have to know to make informed and intelligent voting decisions on all of them. Since the early 1970s, there have been more than a thousand recorded votes in the two houses of each Congress (two years), and of course there are many more nonrecorded votes in committee and on the floor.[4] Consequently, members depend on "cue givers" to guide their votes.

Studies of congressional voting cues show that they come from a variety of sources: committee chairs and ranking members; other committee members, particularly "specialists" whose expertise, intelligence, judgment, and ideological compatibility are trusted; a committee majority; committee or personal staff; party leaders or a majority of one's party; same-party members of one's state delegation; organized congressional groups such as the liberal Democratic Study Group and the conservative Republican Study Committee; a majority of the full chamber; and the president. Many studies have found party (in one form or another) to be the most important cue giver.[5] However, a study done for the House Commission on Administrative Review concluded that personal staff was the single most frequently used source of voting cues.[6] But whatever cue givers a member of Congress makes use of, the sheer number of recorded votes means that political "mistakes" are inevitable.[7]

Members' reliance on voting cues clearly enhances the role of committees. When a committee is relatively united in reporting a bill to the floor and nonmembers of the committee believe that the issue is of little concern to constituents, they are likely to support the committee. This deference to unified committees leads to a taking of turns as clientele of various committees are accommodated, and this taking of turns, while not assuring proportional outcomes, at least partly meets the standards of adversary democracy through protection of a variety of interests. The interests of farmers, small businessmen, veterans, and those benefiting from public works projects have been directly satisfied in this way. When coalition building, reciprocity, and acceptance of voting cues allow policy and prestige committees to be successful, many more groups take turns in getting benefits; groups regularly benefiting from this type of policy making have included bankers, organized labor, educational institutions, state and municipal governments, welfare recipients, the elderly, the unemployed, hospitals, and the many groups that benefit from tax deductions, credits, and exemptions.

With respect to unitary democracy, it is clearly unrealistic to expect 435 representatives and 100 senators to engage in extended deliberation about the common-interest aspects of all the matters that come before them. Even if that were their primary goal, which it is not, senators and representatives simply could not do that because of the number of issues they must deal with and their other responsibilities. This situation produces a necessary departure from three important aspects of unitary democracy: a legislator-legislator focus, equality of status and respect, and a regular striving for consensus. Conflicts in society and in Congress make a search for consensus on most issues impractical. The division of labor evident in the committee system, an institutional response to the congressional workload, produces differences of responsibility and power that make equal status and respect difficult to attain. The variety of activities members feel they must take on and the volume of legislation to be processed limit dependence on interaction between legislators. Members rely on staff, for example, to facilitate compromise and agreement among themselves.

Unanimous Consent and Cloture

Because the Senate lacks a committee to perform the functions of the House Rules Committee, it schedules much of its legislation by unanimous consent agreements. These agreements, which are worked out by majority and minority party leaders and interested senators, establish guidelines for floor deliberations. They set rules for debate, limit debate on various motions, and specify a date for a vote on a bill's final passage. Unlike House Rules Committee rules, which can limit or prohibit amendments to bills, Senate unanimous consent agreements do not limit amendments, with the frequent exception of amendments not germane to the bill under consideration. These agreements require the unanimous approval of all members on the floor at the time. Since leaders of both parties work together and consult all interested senators in negotiating these agreements, every senator with an interest in debating and amending the bill, whether on the relevant committee or not, is given an opportunity to do so.

This wide participation has been even further bolstered by changing Senate customs. The norms of the 1950s, which limited new and junior members to a kind of apprenticeship and discouraged them from speaking both in committee and on the floor and from taking an active role in the floor consideration of bills outside their committee jurisdictions, no longer apply to the Senate of the 1980s.[8] The openness to amendment by committee members and nonmembers on the Senate floor reflects a permeability in Senate decision making not seen to the same extent in the larger House.[9] This suggests a stronger adversary democracy in the Senate than in the House. Interests that were ignored, downplayed, or discounted in committee may be represented on the floor by any senator. Equally important, this can lead committees to take into account more interests at the earlier stage of the legislative process. The greater permeability of the Senate's decision-making process gives senators more opportunity to influence legislation beyond that coming from their own committees. As a result, senators are in a better position to further constituents' interests than representatives are. This, too, strengthens adversary democracy in the Senate relative to the House. While Senate permeability can facilitate more equal power and outcomes more proportional to numbers, it clearly does not assure this, for senators are most likely to use their influence on behalf of those with the resources to communicate their interests most strongly.[10]

Paradoxically, the Senate facilitates adversary democracy through a decision-making process that has many of the attributes of unitary democracy. In establishing guidelines for floor consideration through unanimous consent agreements, the Senate creates an equality of status and uses a consensual approach, which are associated with unitary democracy. In contrast, the House determines rules for floor debate by an often adversary and partisan vote on the rule proposed by the Rules Committee.

The greater openness and permeability of the Senate's decision-making process also has implications for that chamber's unitary democratic capacities. Senators have opportunities to raise broad considerations in a variety of settings, which the typical representative lacks. House members' influence is much more narrowly limited to issues within their committees' jurisdictions. Senators, of course, can use their greater freedom either to raise broader issues than did the reporting committee or to pursue more parochial concerns. Because scholars of Congress have been cautious in distinguishing parochial from national concerns, there are no systematic studies of the direction in which senators actually use their opportunities.

Another aspect of floor procedures in which the Senate and House differ is the use of cloture as a way of ending debate, particularly those extended debates and discussions, known as filibusters, that are used to postpone or avoid voting on certain bills. When there is intense conflict among members, the Senate sometimes cannot agree on a unanimous consent procedure establishing conditions of debate and the date for a vote on final passage. To deal with such cases, the Senate in 1917 adopted its Rule 22, which provided for limitation of debate, or "cloture," if supported by two-thirds of the senators present and voting. In 1975, the rule was changed to allow cloture to be invoked by three-fifths of the Senate, or 60 members. Once cloture has been voted, no senator may speak for more than an hour, only germane amendments may be considered, and the presiding officer may rule dilatory motions out of order. The Senate modified Rule 22 again in 1979 to include in the one-hour limit on each senator after cloture all time spent on parliamentary devices to stall legislative action, such as quorum calls or repeated requests for roll-call votes. This was done after several senators had used such maneuvers to engage in postcloture filibusters.

Even though cloture may be proposed soon after a bill is brought to the floor, senators value the tradition of extended debate and rarely use it that way.[11] Indeed, it is not easy to get 60 senators to vote for cloture at any time, and so proponents of a bill often must decide whether to compromise in order to end a filibuster or the threat of one. Thus the tradition of respect for extended debate gives great power to individual senators and provides a protection for minority interests that is lacking in the House. By the same token, these procedures make it harder for a majority to rule in the Senate. Whether this tends toward an equalization of power, a criterion of adversary democracy, is open to debate and perhaps varies from case to case.

Cloture means that more than majority support is required on issues regarded as particularly important to the common interest. While consensus in the pure sense is neither sought nor attained, more than majority agreement is required. Pressure to modify proposals to come to some agreement are greater than they would be under a simple majority-vote procedure.

Deliberation and Debate

When people visit the Senate, they often see only a very few senators on the floor. Even intense debates frequently involve only a few senators who have particular interest in the legislation. As Sen. Ernest F. Hollings, D-S.C., once observed: "We get in here working hot and heavy in debate, but there is no one here to listen." [12] Staff members often look through the transcripts of debate available in the *Congressional Record* the next day, but it is doubtful much of the content of the debate gets to senators that way. While senators usually can get unanimous consent to speak any time about any topic, whether or not germane to the bill on the floor, they may find themselves speaking to only a few senators, who are there to debate something else and are not very interested in other subjects.

Floor debate in the House is similar in some respects to that in the Senate. Usually only about 20 to 40 members are present, and most of them are members of the committee presenting the bill. When bells ring for a quorum or roll call, more representatives arrive on the floor, but they often leave again after they have voted or registered their presence. Sometimes, they remain on the floor or in a nearby cloakroom after a vote, as when, for example, there is to be a rapid series of votes on amendments. Representatives remaining on the floor usually do not sit quietly listening to debate but instead socialize and engage in informal conversations, perhaps about the issue at hand or perhaps about something completely different. This is a time when members can learn more about the questions before them or other issues that may be coming up. Representatives also learn about the reactions to issues of constituencies other than their own when they talk with colleagues. These informal contacts are therefore an important part of the voting-cue system. When members find that trusted colleagues differ with them on an issue, they may be prompted to further investigation and to contacts with other representatives. In some cases, representatives arrive so late for a vote on an amendment they are unfamiliar with that they only have time to get a cue from a committee member or party leader at the door or from quickly scanning the electronic voting screen. That informal contacts on and off the floor are considered useful is clear in these comments by two representatives:

> If [an issue] hasn't come up at our [state party delegation] breakfast, I'll run to a guy on the floor just about the time the bill is being considered and say, "Hey, what is this all about and what does it do?" And frequently we'll check with the doorkeeper . . . who has a pipeline into the leadership and into those committee members who are responsible for it. . . . A staff member [has] not been exposed to the various pressure groups or the "gut" arguments for or against something. I think the congressman himself involved in that area, who's been on the firing line, can give you a much better capsule than the more isolated staff man.
>
> If I go to the floor to vote in about five minutes on a bill that I've never studied, out of a committee that I'm not familiar with, I have on that committee always several personal friends; they're guys whose judgment I trust or general philosophy of government is the same as mine. We vote alike most of the time and I have a very strong feeling that if I had been on that committee and spent the months and years they have, I know them well enough that I would probably come out about the same point they do. So in these cases that may involve something in which my constituents have no interest, and I'm not familiar with, I will say, "What's the wise vote here? Give me a 30-second briefing on the issues," and then go along.[13]

Floor debates nevertheless serve a variety of functions. They are part of a bill's legislative history, which is often of importance to courts and to government officials who are attempting to determine congressional intent. The debates also provide material for the media and help Congress accomplish its task of education. Sometimes, a debate will bring an issue to national attention and mobilize public sentiment, as has happened with civil rights, the Vietnam War, arms limitation, the Panama Canal treaty, and school prayer.

Thus, debate and extensive presentation of diverse viewpoints with most members present and listening is a rare event in either house of Congress. What is seen, rather, is a kind of catch-as-catch-can deliberation, on and off the floor, involving members, their staffs, executive officials, interest groups, and other constituents. For most issues, systematic deliberation is more likely to occur at the committee stage. This is a problem to the extent that committees are unrepresentative of the chamber. On the other hand, members of Congress who come to the floor to vote are not novices. They have come to Washington with positions, in the form of general stances or specific commitments. They have been exposed to the problems and wishes of constituents. Since most issues have been around before, deliberation may be done in an abbreviated form ("What's changed since last time? Who's changed?"). The give and take between members and constituents, interest groups, and staff, within staffs, and between committee members and nonmembers can all involve deliberation, even if not in an ideal form.

Sometimes deliberation seems to be short-circuited, as when senators or representatives, obliged to vote on an unfamiliar issue, make their decision on the basis of cues from colleagues. When members find themselves disagreeing with normally trusted cue givers or agreeing with those they normally oppose, they may attempt to identify the reasons for the unusual situation, and in so doing they may engage in an abbreviated form of deliberation. When they try to decide what to do when cross-pressured, they also engage in deliberation. Members discuss issues regularly with colleagues whose value preferences they share, as occurs in the Republican policy committees in both the House and the Senate.[14] When they try to determine how to explain a vote to constituents in the limited time they usually have for such explanations, they may be deliberating. When they give attention to the positions of party leaders, a party majority, same-party committee leaders, state party delegations, the president, respected colleagues from the reporting committee, and groups such as the Democratic Study Group and the Republican Study Committee, they can be involved in a deliberative process. Thus, well-attended and closely followed floor debate is not the sole or even the primary form of congressional deliberation.

But the various forms of deliberation are not equally suited to all purposes. From an adversary perspective, members need to communicate and protect the interests of their constituents, learn about those of their colleagues', and if possible move to a practical resolution of conflicting claims. From a unitary perspective, the task is to recognize common interests and move to satisfy them. The problem is in deciding what reasonable standard of deliberation representatives can be held to and what is lost when deliberation is short-circuited or abbreviated. As one House veteran put it, the cue system "can lead to polarized ideological groupings and group voting, not thinking. It can prevent Congress from being a deliberative body involving compromise, the give and take of congressmen, and getting around problems"—suggesting that there are limits on the attainment of both types of democracy in Congress. The possibilities of seeing common interests are constrained by limits on common deliberation.[15] This is not to say that such deliberation would remove all irreconcilable conflicts. Furthermore, only a limited amount of common deliberation can be expected in bodies of 100 and 435 members, each with a huge workload. Finally, deliberation that might improve matters from an adversary perspective does not always produce what is in the common interest. For example, some would argue that the Senate, because it is smaller, should be able to deal with some problems in a way that the House cannot, but whether the Senate does a better job in terms of the common interest is questionable.

The Role of Political Parties

Sometimes, committees and subcommittees form alliances with the clientele they serve and the agencies administering their programs, alliances so powerful they have been called "subgovernments" or "iron triangles."[16] One mechanism that has the potential to control such subgovernments is the political party.[17] The role that parties play also has significance for unitary and adversary democracy.

While parties have been declining in importance, both as bases of voter identification and as electoral organizations bringing members to Congress, they still play important roles in both respects.[18] For example, party-line voting in the election of representatives has decreased over the past three decades, but it is still the case that over two-thirds of those voters who do identify with a party vote for that party's congressional candidate.[19] Numerous congressional voting studies have found party affiliation to be the most important predictor of roll-call votes.[20] It is not hard to see some of the reasons for these findings. For the voter, parties offer a way to make reasonable choices among candidates without incurring excessive information costs. For members of Congress, parties are often the strongest basis for building a coalition that can get legislation passed.

There are differences in the groups that parties tend to represent, differences which are generally sensed by citizens and are evident in general programmatic differences between them. Democrats have tended to support social welfare programs, public-works jobs programs, redistributive tax policies, and government regulation of business. Republicans have been more likely to support reduced government spending for domestic programs and policies that favor higher-income groups and business rather than labor. Republicans have worried more about inflation, Democrats about unemployment.[21] Consequently, voters traditionally associated with the Democratic party have been those with lower incomes, renters rather than homeowners, blacks, those without a college education, city dwellers, and blue-collar workers, whereas the Republican base generally consists of higher-income, home-owning, white, older, college-educated, suburban, and white-collar voters.[22]

While parties are forces of cohesion in both chambers, party leaders in Congress have only limited control over their colleagues. For example, even though leaders of both parties have been well represented on the committees that make committee assignments, they have not attempted to exercise much influence over the vast majority of assignment decisions; instead, they have tried to accommodate most members' requests.[23] In fact, except for the Speaker's power to nominate Democratic members of the House Rules Committee, party leaders do not have sole control of the assignment process. The fact that party leaders have multiple goals, and not just the goal of assuring the political reliability of committees, has also limited their leverage.[24] Only an egregious lack of party loyalty has caused a member to be deprived of a committee position. Phil Gramm, then a Democratic representative from Texas, lost his seat on the House Budget Committee in 1983, not only because he supported the conservative coalition in voting for the Reagan budget and tax cuts of 1981, but because he even helped lead that coalition against the majority of his own party. But the primary emphasis in both parties has been on making committee assignments that would maintain party harmony.[25]

The activity of party leaders in coordinating and intervening in committee affairs is equally limited.[26] The party leadership coordinates demands for floor action, which it must do in its scheduling and political capacity, but it almost never sets guidelines for committees and rarely attempts to resolve intracommittee factional disputes. In every Congress, there are a few issues regarded as sufficiently critical to the party's electoral fortunes or to the president's program to warrant leadership involvement at the committee stage, but leaders are often unable to overcome strong opposing pressures from members' constituencies. While in theory they could affect members' influence and ability to achieve policy goals by taking away committee assignments, they have been unwilling to do that and they know that their colleagues would not permit it. Party leaders depend on the good will and accommodating spirit of committee members to accomplish their own ends.

It is also considered improper for party caucuses to act like committees. On a couple of recent occasions when the House Democratic Caucus passed policy resolutions (one in 1975 opposing military aid to Cambodia and Vietnam and one in 1978 opposing a social security tax increase), there was a strong negative reaction by opponents within the party and by House leaders, which led the caucus to retreat.[27] In the early 1980s, the caucus closed its meetings to the public and did become a forum for policy and strategy discussions, but it has continued to refrain from instructing committees, telling members how to vote on specific matters, and making collective judgments for the party.[28]

The reforms of the 1970s, especially those in the House, reduced the power of committee chairs by making them more responsive to the caucus, which must now vote on them (the Democratic caucus voted out three committee chairs in 1975 and one in 1985), and to the members of their committees, especially majority members. The power that Democrats gave the Speaker to nominate party members of the Rules Committee further strengthened leadership control over scheduling and debate. At the same time, because of these reforms, committee leaders cannot "deliver" committees the way some earlier chairs could, so that chairs are less useful allies of the leadership. Because members can now become subcommittee chairs much earlier in their careers, they are less dependent on party leaders for positions of influence. The reforms also increased the number of recorded votes and opened up committee meetings, both of which reduced the leverage of the parties and their leaders by making it easier for constituents and interest groups to bring pressure to bear.

If there is one area where the parties have the potential for at least temporary dominance over committees, it is in the new congressional budget process. In 1981, under the leadership of the Reagan administration, a Republican Senate majority, and a conservative coalition of Republicans and southern Democrats in the House, Congress voted to instruct authorizing committees to change programs in order to achieve extensive budget cuts. Both the resolution that passed and an unsuccessful one offered as a Democratic alternative specified cuts that forced the committees to make changes in certain programs. Thus, the budget process provides a way to bring about substantial changes in programs.

With that exception, however, congressional parties and their leaders continue to be quite limited in the discipline they are able to exercise. Their reluctance to take control of the committee assignment process, their respect for members' representational obligations, their emphasis on party harmony through accommodation of members' requests, and their restricted ability to affect members' achievement of their goals all contribute to this limitation.

That the two parties are neither united nor disciplined enhances adversary democracy in certain respects. Individual, group, and district interests can be more easily protected in a system of decentralized parties. The legislator-constituency focus is strengthened when members have greater freedom of voting and representation. On the other hand, the lobbying resources, campaign contributions, intensity of conviction, and voter mobilization capacity of certain groups puts them in a position to have more power and receive more than proportional benefits when party discipline is weak. As one member put it, "It takes less to pick off individual members in committee or on the floor than it would to win the support of one of two large, disciplined national parties."

Schattschneider has advanced the thesis that political parties and their leaders are forces that can "socialize" conflict in the American political system, by which he means widening its scope so that a larger audience is aware of and involved in it. As a conflict comes to include a larger audience, both the balance of power and the political outcome often change. Interest groups that can dominate in a small arena, such as a committee, are not as likely to prevail in the larger arenas that are the province of party politics. Since Schattschneider regards government as properly involved in protecting the weak against the strong, in particular against powerful economic interests, he considers this widening of the scope of conflict, and the role of political parties as its instruments, in a positive light. In terms of the present analysis, Schattschneider is arguing that the socializing of conflict would strengthen adversary democracy by facilitating more equal power, more equal protection of interests, and more proportional outcomes.[29]

But because parties are relatively weak in Congress, they are limited in controlling interest-group influence, and their capacity to further the equality required by adversary democracy is consequently also limited. Moreover, it is doubtful that even two large, disciplined parties would drastically limit the influence of major national interest groups, such as organized labor. On the other hand, smaller groups that now have substantial influence in limited areas probably would not have it to the same degree in a system with stronger parties. Thus, more groups are represented under the present system than might be the case with stronger parties, a positive factor by adversary standards; but interests are not protected equally and this inequality is substantial, and these are weaknesses by the same standards.

Because the parties lack discipline, majority coalitions must often be formed issue by issue. Party ranks may provide a large segment of the majority that party leaders seek, but they frequently do not provide sufficient numbers to form a majority by themselves, and leaders must therefore try to win over various groups of members, a process that furthers the representation of diverse interests. One way in which majority coalitions are formed is through what has been called the "politics of inclusion." [30] In this strategy, the benefits of legislation are spread around to include enough congressional districts to assure passage. One problem that results is that benefits are then provided to districts that do not need them, diluting the purpose of the program and making it more expensive. As Arnold has argued, when parties were stronger and able to arrange reciprocal agreements among factions, support on one bill could be traded for support on another to produce a variety of bills, each of which aided a particular constituency on the basis of need. This obviated the need for a politics of inclusion and produced a more rational distribution of benefits.[31] Insofar as the politics of inclusion leads to an allocation of constituency benefits independent of need, it serves well neither adversary democracy nor the common interest.

While each of the major parties exhibits some ideological diversity, which is desirable from both adversary and unitary perspectives, each of them also has (as already noted) a general ideological tendency that reflects a more or less distinctive conception, or cluster of conceptions, of the public interest.[32] Since the two parties disagree about the common interest and how to attain it, they are often in an adversary situation and, as a result, rarely strive for the consensus or broad agreement that characterizes unitary democracy. However, within each congressional party is a core group that sometimes acts as a unitary subsystem. This group strives for wide internal agreement and tries to form a successful majority coalition by reaching agreement with others on the common interest with regard to a particular issue or by fashioning a compromise it does not necessarily feel to be in the national interest.

Congressional parties can also contribute to the unitary goals of policy coordination (making policies consistent in their aims) and fiscal coordination (making expenditure decisions in light of anticipated revenue). Given the decentralization and fragmentation of power in Congress, policy coherence and coordination are obvious, but not always politically advantageous goals, for inconsistent policies may be desirable as, for example, a way of serving diverse constituencies and goals. Some observers have concluded that there is, indeed, too much policy incoherence in congressional output. Because of the parties' limited involvement in committee decision making, they are not in a good position to achieve policy coherence; by the time committees report legislation to the floor, it is usually too late to achieve policy coordination. Even if party leaders tried to achieve it, it is doubtful they could succeed in view of members' independence, except perhaps on very high priority matters and with support by a president of the same party. Party leaders have been somewhat more successful in producing fiscal coordination, but there are political factors that work against this as well (for further discussion, see chapter 8).

In recent years, a number of informal groups have emerged in Congress that may provide partial substitutes for parties.[33] There are currently more than 40 such groups, including the Democratic Study Group (whose members now constitute a majority of House Democrats), the Congressional Black Caucus, the Northeast-Midwest Congressional Coalition (nearly a majority of the entire House), the Congressional Steel Caucus, the Textile Caucus, and the Environmental Study Conference. These groups form alternative channels of information for members, which gives them some independence from both committee and party sources. They also furnish bases for mobilization on various issues and some leverage within the party and the chamber.

These informal groups serve both adversary and unitary ends. Since they often further the representation of particular interests, they strengthen the adversary dimension of Congress, sometimes to the point of causing difficulties for the two parties by seeking major concessions as the price of support. On the other hand, they sometimes represent conceptions of the common or national interest that may get short shrift in parties and committees. They can become unitary subsystems in which internal agreement is sought to enhance the groups' leverage in the chamber. On balance, however, these groups seem to serve adversary more than unitary ends. Perhaps because senators are already in a better position to serve those ends, that chamber has not seen the development of as many informal groups as the House has.

Conclusion

The structure and procedures of the Senate provide the basis for a stronger adversary democracy there than in the House. But the House shows a historical movement toward a stronger adversary process both on the floor and in some important committees. In both chambers, the parties appear to strengthen adversary democracy by allowing for the protection of a great variety of interests, but weaken it by their inability to limit unequal power. As is often the case in politics, the weaknesses and strengths are two sides of the same coin. Strengthening the unitary qualities of political parties would therefore probably have a negative effect on their adversary qualities, and vice versa. For example, while more disciplined parties could advance policy coherence and reduce the influence of some special interests, they would not represent other individual and district interests as well as they do now. As a result of the weakening and decentralization of political parties over the last two decades, many particular interests receive better representation, but at the cost of equal protection of interests and policy coherence. Future reforms in the congressional parties would involve similar tradeoffs.

NOTES

1. For an analysis of the struggle to enlarge the committee, see Milton C. Cummings and Robert L. Peabody, "The Decision to Enlarge the Committee on Rules," in *New Perspectives on the House of Representatives*, 2nd ed., ed. Robert L. Peabody and Nelson W. Polsby (Chicago: Rand McNally, 1969), 253-281.
2. The following is based on the insightful analysis of Roger H. Davidson and Walter J. Oleszek, *Congress and Its Members* (Washington, D.C.: CQ Press, 1981), 381-383.
3. Unless otherwise noted, quotes from members in this and later chapters are taken from interviews which the authors held with them between 1975 and 1979.
4. Norman J. Ornstein et al., *Vital Statistics on Congress, 1982* (Washington, D.C.: American Enterprise Institute, 1982), 135.

5. See, for example, Donald R. Matthews and James A. Stimson, *Yeas and Nays: Normal Decision-Making in the U.S. House of Representatives* (New York: Wiley, 1975), 94.
6. House Commission on Administrative Review, *Administrative Reorganization and Legislative Management*, 95th Cong., 1st sess., September 28, 1977, 56-57. The question of how members get and use information is discussed in greater detail in chapter 6.
7. For an illustration of one such "mistake," see the account of the difficulty of former Rep. Joseph Fisher, D-Va., in Davidson and Oleszek, *Congress and Its Members*, 382.
8. David W. Rohde, Norman J. Ornstein, and Robert L. Peabody, "Political Change and Legislative Norms in the United States Senate" (Paper delivered at the annual meeting of the American Political Science Association, Chicago, 1974). For a description of the Senate in the 1950s, see Donald R. Matthews, *U.S. Senators and Their World* (New York: Vintage, 1960), 92-102.
9. Richard F. Fenno, Jr., *Congressmen in Committees* (Boston: Little, Brown, 1973), 139-191.
10. Of course, senators, like representatives, sometimes attempt to cultivate constituencies and in so doing can represent and even mobilize interests that are latent. Entrepreneurial staff members may also lead them to promote ideas and issues that currently lack strong constituency bases. However, it is doubtful that these forces are sufficiently strong to balance the tendency to represent most vigorously the best organized interests.
11. Walter J. Oleszek, *Congressional Procedures and the Policy Process* (Washington, D.C.: CQ Press, 1978), 169-170.
12. *Wall Street Journal*, September 17, 1973, 10, cited in Oleszek, *Congressional Procedures*, 156.
13. Matthews and Stimson, *Yeas and Nays*, 24 and 91.
14. Charles O. Jones, *The United States Congress: People, Place, Policy* (Homewood, Ill.: Dorsey, 1982), 304.
15. This is developed further in chapter 6.
16. See Ernest S. Griffith, *The Impasse of Democracy* (Harrison, N.Y.: Hilton, 1939), 182; Douglass Cater, *Power in Washington* (New York: Random House, 1964); and J. Lieper Freeman, *The Political Process* (New York: Random House, 1965). Hugh Heclo, "Issue Networks and the Executive Establishment," in *The New American Political System*, ed. Anthony King (Washington, D.C.: American Enterprise Institute, 1982), 102, has argued that congressional decision making is so permeable and relationships in policy making so fluid and complex that the metaphor of "iron triangle" is misleading. He prefers the term "issue networks." This alternative conception, however, does not eliminate the problem of the unrepresentativeness of committees or what some see as their excessive catering to organized interests, unchecked by Congress as a whole.
17. E. E. Schattschneider, *The Semisovereign People* (New York: Holt, Rinehart & Winston, 1961).
18. For discussions of the decline of political parties, see Everett C. Ladd, *Where Have All the Voters Gone?* (New York: W. W. Norton, 1978), and William Crotty and Gary Jacobson, *American Parties in Decline* (Boston: Little, Brown, 1980).

19. Thomas E. Mann and Raymond E. Wolfinger, "Candidates and Parties in Congressional Elections," *American Political Science Review* 74 (September 1980): 620.
20. For example, see Julius Turner, *Party and Constituency: Pressures on Congress,* rev. ed., ed. Edward V. Schneier, Jr. (Baltimore: The Johns Hopkins University Press, 1970).
21. William J. Keefe, *Congress and the American People,* 2nd ed. (Englewood Cliffs, N.J.: Prentice-Hall, 1984), 125-126.
22. David J. Vogler, *The Politics of Congress,* 4th ed. (Boston: Allyn & Bacon, 1983), 105.
23. For the House, see Barbara Sinclair, *Majority Party Leadership in the U.S. House* (Baltimore: The Johns Hopkins University Press, 1983), 68-73, and Sidney Waldman, "Majority Leadership in the House of Representatives," *Political Science Quarterly* 95 (Fall 1980): 375. For the Senate, see Robert L. Peabody, *Leadership in Congress* (Boston: Little, Brown, 1976), 349-350.
24. Sinclair, *Majority Party Leadership,* 71.
25. See Steven S. Smith and Christopher J. Deering, *Committees in Congress* (Washington, D.C.: CQ Press, 1984), 242-246. The authors point out, however, that the House Democratic leadership has said that the Democratic members of its four prestige committees would be held to a higher standard of party support than members of other committees and has generally followed that policy since the 95th Congress (1977-1978).
26. Ibid., 248, and Sinclair, *Majority Party Leadership,* 98-108.
27. See Sidney Waldman, "Leadership in the House of Representatives: The 94th and 95th Congresses" (Paper delivered at the annual meeting of the American Political Science Association, Washington, D.C., 1977), 32-36, and Ann Cooper, "Democrats Still Arguing over Party Caucus Role on Legislative Matters," *Congressional Quarterly Weekly Report,* April 15, 1978, 868 and 874-876.
28. See Sinclair, *Majority Party Leadership,* 93-97, and *Congressional Quarterly Weekly Report,* October 15, 1983, 2115-2119.
29. Schattschneider, *Semisovereign People.*
30. R. Douglas Arnold, "The Local Roots of Domestic Policy," in *The New Congress,* ed. Thomas E. Mann and Norman J. Ornstein (Washington, D.C.: American Enterprise Institute, 1981), 285.
31. Ibid., 286.
32. Jerrold E. Schneider, *Ideological Coalitions in Congress* (Westport, Conn.: Greenwood, 1979).
33. For a discussion of these groups, see Roger H. Davidson, "Subcommittee Government: New Channels for Policy Making," in Mann and Ornstein, *New Congress,* 128-131, and Burdett A. Loomis, "Congressional Caucuses and the Politics of Representation," in *Congress Reconsidered,* 2nd ed., ed. Lawrence C. Dodd and Bruce I. Oppenheimer (Washington, D.C.: CQ Press, 1981), 204-220.

Informational Needs and Sources | 6

Gathering and processing information is perhaps the central activity in the operation of Congress. Members regularly use the language of information and communication to describe interactions with constituents, executive officials, staff, and colleagues. Congressional scholars have found that studying the ways in which members of Congress search for and process information is a useful approach to understanding the institution and explaining its decisions.[1] The framework of this book leads to the questions of whether adversary and unitary democracies call for different types of information and whether the adversary and unitary models provide distinctive and useful standards for evaluating the information that members of Congress receive, especially the information received from the internal networks of Congress itself.

Types of Expertise

In her study of the town-meeting government of Selby, Vermont, Mansbridge found that townspeople often linked political participation with information and knowledge. The information and knowledge were associated not only with level of formal education, but also with socioeconomic status or class more generally and with length and location of residence in Selby specifically. Townspeople's modes of participatory behavior—attending town meeting, speaking at the meeting, and holding office—also varied along the same dimensions. For example, newcomers to Selby (those who had lived there less than 12 years) were less likely to attend town meeting than old-timers; middle-class newcomers were not much more likely to attend than working-class newcomers, but middle-class newcomers who did attend were more likely to speak than were working-class newcomers.

Explanations for these and other differences in participation put forward by the residents often referred to knowledge and information. One old-timer, complaining about newcomers in general and a very active newcomer named Gretsch in particular, said: "They think the people around here don't know anything! That Gretsch thinks they need to get out a brochure because no one knows anything about Selby. Well, Selby's been here a good long time and a lot of people know a lot about it!" A machinist who had lived in Selby for 20 years explained why he had never been to town meeting by saying, "I figure to let the people who know more about it run it." An assembly-line worker who was a newcomer said that people like her did not go to town meeting: "A lot of people are not educated enough to understand it." And the holder of a minor office who lived outside of the village said that being away from the close interaction of villagers resulted in his being ignorant on some matters: "There's too much that goes on before town meeting that we don't know about unless we're part of it. They're slack in presenting all the information you need to function completely." [2]

In analyzing the differences both in participation and in justifications for that participation, Mansbridge found that, for newcomers, the informational basis of participation in town government was most often that of professional or technical competence gained through formal education and work experience outside of Selby. For active old-timers, on the other hand, the information relevant to participation was based on their "having known the town intimately since childhood," on long-term ties that "create a fund of politically useful information." [3] This distinction, Mansbridge pointed out, is similar to that made by Max Weber between "rational-legal" and "traditional" bases of legitimacy.

Both types of information are useful to both unitary and adversary democracy, in that they help people to perceive interests and to make policy choices that are "enlightened" preferences. Mansbridge described the relationship between the two types of information and unitary democracy:

> Both the large upper stratum of old-timers and the small upper stratum of newcomers can claim a better than average perception of the common good and better than average capacities for bringing it about. . . .

> The old-timers base their claim on tradition and on their greater-than-average knowledge of the town. . . . Newcomers in the top stratum base their claim on their greater-than-average competence, demonstrated by success in the world outside Selby.[4]

In a later article, Mansbridge pointed out that either kind of "expertise" is important in unitary democracy to the extent that it gives representatives "useful insight into some aspect of the common good."[5]

If expertise is valuable in unitary democracy because it helps decision makers to recognize the common good, the equivalent in adversary democracy consists of skills and knowledge of procedures that enable decision makers to protect their interests against the claims of others. To be successful in an adversary situation, Mansbridge said, one must be "an eloquent speaker, a successful operator, a person who is not easily duped"—a type she referred to as a "gladiator." Recognizing that any decision-making institution will contain both adversary and unitary elements, Mansbridge wrote that what is needed is "experts on issues of common interest and gladiators on issues of conflicting interest."[6]

The distinction between the expertise of professional competence and the skills of the gladiator, however, is not altogether clear. In Selby, the expertise of certain newcomers seemed to have more of an effect on their ability to participate in adversary proceedings than it did on their ability to recognize common interests. The expertise of old-timers, on the other hand, seemed to be of little value in adversary participation.[7] How do we determine when information that is needed by decision makers is expertise or knowledge on the substantive issue before them and when it is procedural expertise or knowledge about decision makers themselves? This is one of the questions to be asked about the use of information in the congressional process. It seems likely that legislators will need different types of information, which they get from different sources and use differently, depending on whether the legislative process is closer to adversary or unitary democracy.

The Context of Congressional Information

A survey conducted by the Joint Committee on the Organization of Congress in 1946 found that the institutional shortcoming most often raised by members of Congress was the inadequate size of professional staff. In its final report, the committee concluded: "The shocking lack of adequate congressional fact-finding services and skilled staffs sometimes reaches such ridiculous proportions as to make Congress dependent upon 'hand-outs' from Government departments and private groups or newspaper stories for its basic fund of information on which to base legislative decisions."[8] The committee recommended enlarging the professional committee staffs and expanding the Legislative Reference Service to overcome this information deficit.

The Legislative Reorganization Act of 1946 incorporated these and other changes, marking the beginning of a dramatic change in congressional staffing and information resources. Between 1947 and 1981, the number of staff members working for congressional committees increased sevenfold, from 399 to 2,865. The increase in the size of the personal staffs of senators and representatives was almost as great. In 1981, there were 11,125 personal staffers in Congress, more than five times the 2,030 who had held such positions in 1947. There was a concomitant expansion in other congressional support agencies. In 1947, the Legislative Reference Service had a staff of 160; in 1981, the reorganized Congressional Research Service employed 849 staff members. Congress also created two new support agencies in the mid-1970s: the Congressional Budget Office and the Office of Technology Assessment, which employed 218 and 130 people, respectively, in 1981.[9] These changes in Congress's informational support system have been characterized by one scholar as an "explosion."[10]

There is no doubt that legislators today have access to more information—and yet, even after this great expansion of information services, members of Congress still cite problems of information as an important concern for legislative decision makers. Both the House and the Senate studied the problems in 1977. A survey of 153 representatives conducted for the House Commission on Administrative Review uncovered "the existence of significant substantive information problems," which were summarized as follows:

> Roughly one-third of the Members interviewed have difficulty assessing the impact of legislation nationally or locally; forty percent have problems securing information concerning existing needs, past efforts, or other proposals when working on committee legislation on the floor that is reported from committees on which they do not sit.[11]

This study found that the problems lay not in the amount of information but rather in its accessibility—its availability in a format and context that made it useful to legislative decision makers. Indeed, one House member commented that "there is no dearth of information, there is a deluge."[12] Another, referring to information provided by the Armed Services Committee, said: "They did send over the hearings. But here it is, 8000 pages long or something like that. How can you go through all that? It's useless to me."[13]

Senators made similar complaints in the course of a study done for the Commission on the Operation of the Senate. One said, for example: "You make an inquiry to the Library of Congress. You get back a stack of volumes that high—that's utterly useless." [14] Two scholars who worked for this commission have written:

> Whenever Senators need or want specific information or data, they can get it—from staff, lobbyists, the Library of Congress, etc. When they think of information, they think of reports of several hundred pages which they have no time to read—of too much information, in other words. They rarely think of unfulfilled needs.
>
> Senators do not feel a lack of information. What they are missing, however, is the ability to place the information they have in broader contexts, and the time to think about the broader questions. Therefore, in analyzing the ability of Senators and the Senate to do in-depth, long range, crosscutting examination of policy alternatives, the distinction must be made between information or data, and knowledge. [15]

Thus, the information problem in Congress has changed from a shortage of data to that of an excess of data. It is ironic that the growth of congressional staff, which came about as a way to improve the information available to legislative decision makers, may even be one of the causes of the current information glut. Malbin has shown how the staff system provides incentives for committee and legislative aides continually to search for and develop legislative proposals and supporting information and arguments. By generating new information, these staff "entrepreneurs" actually add to, rather than reduce, the information problems of members of Congress. [16] Meanwhile, increases in congressional workloads have cut down on the amount of time legislators have for absorbing the information provided to them and for developing their own knowledge of policy areas. Surveys of House members have found that, whereas in 1965, the average work week for a representative included more than seven hours—virtually a full day—for legislative research and reading, the figure had declined to one hour a week in 1977. [17] This is the time when legislators could strive "to place the information they have in broader contexts" and "to think about the broader questions"—the types of activities that legislators must engage in to develop knowledge, instead of merely gathering information.

The distinction between knowledge and information is helpful in understanding the changes that have been described and in analyzing how information is used in legislative decision making. In his study of the impact of computers in Congress, Frantzich defined information as "facts, data, opinions, analysis, and interpretations." It was, he said, "the raw material for knowledge"; conversely, he defined knowledge as "information that has been evaluated, refined, and organized." [18] There is a value component to knowledge and a time element that is required for refinement and organization. Schneier has used the term *intelligence* with the same meaning that Frantzich gave to knowledge: As distinct from information, which is "raw data ... abundant, cheap, easy to acquire, sometimes hard to avoid," intelligence is "processed data, data that has been evaluated and given meaning, is much more difficult to acquire and much more important to have." [19]

Types of Information

The distinction between knowledge and information is not sufficient to capture the complexities of the informational needs of Congress. Even within the category of "raw data," there are different types that are suitable to different purposes. Making unsuitable data available may actually subvert Congress's proper purpose, as King has pointed out:

> The trouble is that large staffs and ready access to knowledge (of a kind) can tempt legislators into imagining that they know more than they really do, into supposing that the knowledge gained from reading reports and questioning witnesses is equivalent to the knowledge gained from practical experience, and, not least, into imagining that they are actually in a position to run a country's administration as distinct from merely helping to keep an eye on it. Large staffs and computers can, in other words, breed a sort of legislative hubris.[20]

Macmahon made a similar point as early as 1943: Too much concern for detailed information on the implementation of policy made Congress less effective as a representative and policy-making institution. "The hazard is that a body like Congress, when it gets into detail, ceases to be itself." [21]

The term *political information* has been used by some students of legislative decision making for the mixture of empirical facts and values that others have referred to as knowledge. Porter, for example, has defined political information as consisting of judgments of "potential impact and statements of preference and position by various interest groups and public officials" and "judgments as to the practicality and feasibility of particular measures as well as the potential impact on local constituencies or the state at large." He contrasted this with *technical information*—straightforward empirical information about the nature of a particular problem, past efforts to deal with it, policy alternatives, and "the content of legislation." [22] A similar distinction can be perceived in this observation:

A congressman needs to know not only what the policy consequences of given votes will be, but also what the political consequences
will be, either in terms of effects in his constituency or in terms of the
reward structure within the House. Useful information, therefore, takes
account of the political consequences, modifies the information in light
of those consequences, and becomes politically realistic. . . .

Observers often note the need for congressmen to have "neutral"
information that is not tainted with vested interest or other bias.
Actually, such neutral information is much less useful than information
which takes a position and buttresses the argument with selected
facts.[23]

It has been suggested that "neutral" or technical information and
political information may be mutually exclusive:

The more information is processed, the greater its utility for a
Member of Congress. However, the problem is that the more that
information is processed, the greater the possibility of distortion, so
that one is faced with the paradox that the best kind of information that
a Member can have is also the least likely to be free of distortion.
Without intending to be cynical, I would argue that the best possible
intelligence you can get is a reliable directive to vote yes or no. The
problem is the word "reliable." The more complicated the legislative
issue, the more difficult is that problem of reliability. The worst kind of
information you can have is 5,000 pages stuck on your desk with no
evaluation.[24]

More moderately, legislators have been urged to "distance" themselves
from technical information:

The question of the price at which oil can be extracted from shale is
a technical question; the question of whether oil should be extracted at
that price, of the associated costs and benefits for society at large, is a
political question. Legislators who seek to turn themselves into technical experts are likely to fail at that task, and they are likely at the same
time to cease to translate complex issues into terms that lay persons can
understand [resulting in] a potential loss of democratic legitimacy, with
legislators ceasing to function as politicians.[25]

Frantzich has devised an even more refined classification of information relevant to congressional decision making. It consists of the
following types:

1. *Decision-making*—empirical data relevant to a definition of the
policy problem, the alternative courses of action, and their projected
consequences (in essence, what others call technical information)

2. *Political*—a combination of empirical information and evaluation,
which seeks "to link facts with the values underlying political choices"

3. *Monitoring*—information on the status of all pending legislation, such as is provided by the Legislative Information System

4. *Strategy*—scheduling information (when a bill is expected to be reported out of committee and brought up on the floor) and information on members' voting intentions and the probabilities of changing them

5. *Oversight*—data on the administration of programs and the implementation of policy, most of which is provided by executive departments and agencies

6. *Constituency*—data on the opinions of constituents, as reflected in mail and other forms of communication, and objective data on the impact of existing or proposed federal programs and projects on the district or state

7. *Administrative*—organizational information on members and on the more than 30,000 people working for Congress, including such matters as their work schedules and publications, information storage and retrieval, and physical plant operations[26]

Such classifications help explain why some members and students of Congress lament that decision makers often lack essential information while others talk about an information overload: A decision-making organization may have more than enough of one type of information and at the same time be short of other types. These classifications, by distinguishing among types of information, also suggest that different types and sources of information may have varying degrees of importance at different stages of the legislative process, and they raise questions about the type of information people must have if their preferences among policy choices are to be "enlightened" ones.

Stages of Policy Making

So far as the need for different types of information is concerned, it is useful to consider three stages of the policy-making process: agenda setting, formulation, and legitimation.[27]

Agenda Setting

Two types of activities go into determining the policy agenda: the perception and definition of problems regarded as appropriate for government solutions, and the ordering of those problems in terms of priorities. Technical information, or what Frantzich called decision-making information, is needed to place items on the agenda, although oversight information and constituency information can also lead policy makers to perceive problems that should be put on the agenda. Determining priorities among agenda items, however, requires political information as well. Empirical data on the effects of acid rain on forests and water supplies, for example, might suggest that the problem is severe enough to put it on the agenda, but its priority ranking will depend on political information—on evaluative determinations of costs and benefits to different sectors of society, of electoral consequences, and of the importance of other agenda items.

In his 1960 book on presidential power, Richard Neustadt observed: "Congressmen need an agenda from outside, something with high status to respond to or react against. What provides it better than the program of the President?" [28] While the president's program still influences the order of priorities on the agenda (a clear example was the domination of the agenda in 1981 and 1982 by President Reagan's spending and tax programs), members of Congress now have the resources and technical information to initiate action on certain issues and thus to have a greater impact on the agenda than they did at the time Neustadt wrote. Twenty years later, Ripley and Franklin were able to say:

> Congress can and does get involved in initiation on a broad range of issues. For example, Congress was responsible for initiation in the following policy areas in recent years: Medicare, Social Security disability insurance, pension reform, the 18-year-old vote, political campaign reform, air pollution (including automobile pollution), reduction and cessation of the U.S. role in the Indochina war, chemical additives in foods, the creation of a consumer protection agency, mandatory automobile safety standards, food programs for the poor, and increases in the minimum wage.[29]

It is particularly the growth of professional staffs in Congress and their "entrepreneurial" style that has produced this change.[30] These professional staff members regularly interact with interest-group and executive professionals and bring information and new ideas from those networks into Congress. Members of Congress respond to at least some of this information and these ideas by adding new items to the agenda and by introducing legislation and generating interest in and support for the new issues.

Fenno has suggested that, in developing a policy agenda, American legislators operate as inductive thinkers: "They start with a specific, frequently constituency-related instance and get a handle on what is going on in the executive branch. They then work inductively from that very concrete, detailed event, moving outward and upward toward more general policy statements." [31] Oversight and constituency information brought to the congressional office is the raw material in such an inductive process. These types of information serve at this stage not as conclusive proof of why a particular approach or program is the best solution, but rather as evidence to support placing an issue on the congressional agenda. Nonlegislative casework and constituency services performed by members' personal staffs can trigger the inductive process, while technical information and "details" produced in the course of overseeing administration can lead, by the same process, to proposals for new programs and modifications of existing programs.

Formulation

The number of actors involved in agenda setting and the nature of the congressional process create a multiplicity of program and policy proposals in each issue area. The formulation stage of the policy-making process consists of research and analysis of the options in a particular area and evaluation of and selection among alternatives. Formulation is likely to involve executive specialists and political officials and private-sector representatives, as well as members of Congress and their staff assistants. The congressional hearing is the most public arena of policy formulation and the committee report (including the committee bill) its most visible product.

It would be expected that technical information plays an important part in the formulation stage. The presence of policy alternatives and the political considerations associated with these alternatives, however, lead to biases and selectivity in its use at this stage. It is used not only to show the existence of a problem but also to support a particular solution to it.

In a study of policy formulation in the executive branch, Paul Light found that "the first questions asked of alternatives act as evaluative screens through which all potential programs must pass." [32] In the Kennedy and Johnson administrations, the first questions asked about policy alternatives were most often those about the political costs. In the Nixon, Ford, and Carter administrations, questions about economic costs were found to come first. Questions about the workability of programs, the technical costs, were much less important than those concerning economic or political costs in all five administrations. The nature of the initial focus would determine the type of information regarded as crucial.

Similarly, it would be expected that the type of information that is useful at the formulation stage in Congress will also depend on whether the evaluation of alternatives is dominated by economic, political, or technical considerations. For example, information about the workability of immigrant amnesty programs or of sanctions against employers who hire illegal aliens may be less important at this stage than political information on the likely support in Congress for different programs. However, the increase in the "uncontrollable" share of the budget and the consequent decline in federal spending flexibility is bound to also affect policy formulation in Congress (and in the executive branch as well). Questions about the costs of alternative policy proposals would therefore influence the search for information.

A number of characteristics associated with the policy formulation stage support extensive use of quantitative data. Information expressed in this form can appear to be a result of objective research and analysis, and the selective use of such data can give a tactical advantage to one side in a debate on alternative policies. As a reporter has said:

> Capitol Hill feeds on numbers, some authoritative, some spurious, to buttress arguments and gain votes. Even when the numbers are conflicting they often become the focus of a debate in Congress, setting its [parameters] and sometimes determining the outcome. . . . The person with the numbers sets the tone of the discussion, and his figures have to be debunked before his argument can be refuted.[33]

Nevertheless, there may well be an underlying subjectivity in this seemingly objective data. Observation of the congressional debate in 1977-1978 on deregulation of natural-gas prices led Malbin to comment:

> Countless "analyses" of the consumer costs and supply benefits of price deregulation were produced by committee staffs and support agencies and then cited in committee and on the floor. Each was based on its own mathematical model. The quantitative conclusions about costs and benefits were tossed around by members with great authority and were suitably headlined in the press.
>
> Whatever their rhetorical utility, however, the studies in fact were of little intellectual benefit. Every one of them had to assume answers to questions that were really ones of geology, international relations, antitrust law, and political philosophy. If the members had understood, debated, and at least tentatively answered all of those questions, they would have had all they needed to decide how to vote—without the models. The models added nothing new to this debate, largely because their quantitative conclusions followed directly from the more important non-quantitative premises.[34]

Congressional staffs supply members of Congress with most of the quantitative data that are used to evaluate policy alternatives. Malbin found that committee staffs in the Senate, and to an increasing degree in the House, were also responsible for much of the negotiation between proponents of different policy proposals.[35] Thus, staffs participate in the formulation stage not only by performing research and analysis but also by helping to select among the policy alternatives.

Finally, it should be pointed out that information needed to place an issue on the policy agenda comes primarily from sources outside Capitol Hill, as a response to a perceived problem in society, whereas information needed at the policy formulation stage is more likely to have been generated within Congress.

Legitimation

Specific activities included in the legitimation stage are identification of interests, communication among those interests, bargaining, and compromise. These activities take place both in committee and on the floor, but since a bill ultimately requires appoval by a majority in each chamber, the focus here will be on congressional floor action.

The types of information most important to members at the legitimation stage are political, strategy, and constituency, with their relative importance depending on the policy under consideration and the distribution of support among the membership. The sources of information that are of greatest importance at this stage are fellow senators and representatives.[36] One veteran House member has said: "You vote with others whom you trust and whom you feel have had time for deliberation, and whose views are generally in line with yours. Sometimes you stagger into the room, you don't even know what they're voting on. How did George vote? Okay. . . . The deliberative time is such as is required to see how someone else voted." [37]

One reason why colleagues are important sources of information at this stage is that the type of information needed is more likely to be political than technical. Legitimation involves the identification of interests, which goes beyond the cognizance of an issue or an awareness of alternative policy proposals. Members need the kind of information that links facts with the values underlying the choices before them, and colleagues are more likely to be good sources of information on the interests and values involved in a decision than staff members are. A representative has observed: "A staff member is reading the cold lifeless reports. They have not been exposed to the various pressure groups or the gut arguments for or against something. I think the congressman himself involved in that area, who's been on the firing line, can give you a much better capsule than the more isolated staff man." [38]

The cue system, on which members rely heavily for information relevant to floor voting, is a highly differentiated one. Initial cue givers, who bring information from outside Congress, include committee leaders with expertise in a particular area. Intermediary cue givers are a member's colleagues, including the state party delegation and other party and ideological groups, who pass along information that is more evaluative and political. It is how particular members feel about a bill on the floor, their recommendation based on a political judgment, that is of greatest use to other members who are deciding how to vote.

Other reasons for legislators' reliance on colleagues for voting cues are their shared characteristics and common membership in a peer group; common experience of campaigning and election; knowledge and insights as professional politicians; regular and repeated opportunities for evaluating each other's attitudes and actions; differences in presence on and absence from the floor during votes; and the ability to hold colleagues accountable in future votes.[39] Most importantly, members look to other members for information they simply cannot get elsewhere. Malbin argues that "indirect staff mediation and communication by memorandum" are not sufficient because they "cannot help a member *feel* or *sense* his colleagues' reactions to his own or each other's arguments." [40] He goes on to say that this type of information is essential to (unitary) democracy: "In a democratic government, based on the acceptance and presumed trust of the people, whether a program (or the rhetoric used to support a program) induces massive resentment, passive acceptance, or warm endorsement may be every bit as important as any of its other effects." [41] In adversary democracy, face-to-face political interaction is a check on elite coercion.

Information and the Two Democracies

The relationship between the informational requirements of different stages of the congressional policy-making process and the types of information best suited to adversary and unitary democracy invites comparison and discussion. The analysis may be instructive about both congressional policy making and the two forms of democracy.

Information for Adversary Democracy

The central principle of adversary democracy is the equal protection of interests. The model of the adversary process most evident in the American legal system and embodied in the Constitution rests on the premise that the adversary process will generate the fullest possible range of information relevant to a decision.

Members of Congress achieve their positions through a selection process based on adversary principles. Furthermore, approximately half of the members are lawyers. It is no surprise, therefore, to find that members are comfortable with the sort of reasoning associated with the adversary process and that they favor an adversary approach to information gathering, in which one searches for information that will support a particular position rather than undertaking a comprehensive search for objective data before arriving at a position. The belief that the adversary process itself will generate all relevant information removes or reduces the individual legislator's responsibility for obtaining objective and complete information.[42]

The information needed for adversary purposes is routinely provided by elements of the congressional network. Some congressional committees and personal and committee staff are important sources of this type of information. Initial cue givers such as committee leaders are highly regarded for their expertise, but members often question the value premises shaping the information which these leaders provided to other members.[43] Some committees, such as the agriculture committees in both chambers, are regarded as advocates of certain interests or policies, and so the value placed upon the expertise and technical information that they contribute to the legislative process will depend on whether a member shares the committee's outlook.[44]

The personal staffs of members of Congress are another source of information that is important in the adversary process. Because they are likely to share the political values of the senators or representative for whom they work, the information they provide is likely to reflect that value framework.[45] The information that comes from the staff helps gird the legislator for battle; it is a means of reinforcement rather than of enlightenment. Malbin has distinguished between what he calls "personalized" staffs, whose primary loyalty is to a particular senator or representative, and "corporate" staffs, who regard themselves as working for the committee as a whole. He found a growing tendency toward personalized staffs, a trend that not only emphasizes the partisan and adversarial use of information but also leads committee staff members themselves to engage in actual negotiations during the adversary process. Resolution of a conflict through compromise requires that at least some members have information about other members' positions and that they have shared interests, in addition to the information and interests that support their own position. The congressional staff network can provide some of the necessary information and can also serve as bargaining agents for legislators in reaching a compromise.[46]

However, what needs to be emphasized is the limited effect of information in an adversary system. Increasing the amount of information available to decision makers in such a system is unlikely to have any great impact on the outcome. There is little hope, as Frantzich points out, "that increased information will somehow transform politicians into philosopher kings." [47] The Office of Technology Assessment (OTA) arrived at a similar conclusion in 1984 after a four-year study of acid rain. Additional scientific research on the impact of pollutants and the costs of controls would do little to help Congress arrive at a policy in this area, the OTA report said. The information produced by the studies reviewed in the report had the effect of confirming arguments made by both sides in the acid rain debate: Pollutants are indeed a source of great environmental damage, and control costs are high.[48] Policy resolution on this issue will come about as a result of decisions on the relative weights given to economic development and environmental protection and on the geographic distribution of costs. Information relevant to those questions is more likely to be produced by members of Congress engaged in a unitary pattern of interaction.

Information for Unitary Democracy

The central characteristic of unitary democracy, which distinguishes it from adversary democracy, is that policy resolution is achieved on the basis of perceived common interests rather than through a compromise that gives equitable protection to different interests. Mansbridge suggests that there are three ways in which individuals may come to have common interests: their private interests may overlap; empathy may lead them to regard others' interests as their own; and they may share a belief in a certain principle or principles.[49] Consequently, the focus here is on the types of information and information processes that would lead decision makers to become aware of common interests in any of these three ways.

Although congressional staffs can provide members with some information about overlapping interests between groups in one district and groups in other districts or about the degree to which a particular policy proposal meets the standards of equity or some other principle, the most regular source of this type of information seems to be face-to-face contact with other members. Although Mansbridge acknowledges that there is no necessary or logical connection between face-to-face interaction and awareness of these bases of common interests, the nature of the congressional cue system does suggest that, at least for that institution, face-to-face contact is essential. The most extensive cue network in Congress for the transmission of value judgments is made up of intermediary cue givers—members of the state's delegation and party and ideological groups—whose usefulness as a source of cues has been characterized as "questionable expertise based on unquestionable value premises." [50] What members want to know from their colleagues is how to vote on an issue, not what the facts are supporting one side or the other. "I buy their conclusions, not their data," is the way one legislator has put it.[51]

It is this value component of members' cues that facilitates unitary democracy within Congress. The ideological and partisan nature of the intermediary cue network means that members look to colleagues with a similar regard for certain principles and for the application of those principles to the policy under consideration. The face-to-face interaction that helps members to "feel" or "sense" their colleagues' reactions to their own or each other's arguments may be useful in an adversary process as a measure of intensity of opinion and as a way of gaining information that facilitates bargaining and compromise. In a unitary democracy, however, face-to-face interaction in which members get a "sense" of their colleagues' reactions is an absolute necessity. It is the means by which legislators come to perceive overlapping interests, to empathize with colleagues, and to recognize common principles—the means, in other words, by which they come to make decisions on the basis of common interests.

A characteristic of the legislative cue system that seems important to unitary interaction is an underlying pattern of trust. The House Commission on Administrative Review signaled the importance of trust in shaping the legislative information network by making it the first characteristic discussed in its final report: "Loyalty and trust are key ingredients on Capitol Hill. Valid information will be discounted if legislators or staff aides lack trust in the person or organization presenting the material." [52] Members of Congress regularly employ the concept of trust when describing the cue network, as did the former representative quoted earlier—"You vote with others whom you trust"—and as did the representatives interviewed by Matthews and Stimson:

> There are people in whom I have a lot of confidence—I take their word on legislation. I can learn as much in 10 or 15 minutes' conference on the floor with another member that I can trust as I think I would by spending a lot of hours trying to do research on a field in which I have no expertise.

You can't be knowledgeable about every bill that comes up. But *somebody* knows *something* about the bill.... You've got to trust people who know more about a thing because you just don't have enough hours, enough years in your life to learn all you should.

If I go to the floor to vote in about 5 minutes on a bill that I've never studied, out of a committee that I'm not familiar with, I have on that committee always several personal friends; they're guys whose judgment I trust or general philosophy of government is the same as mine.... You have to make a decision on the best basis you can. The best basis is "What do specialists in the field who have my general philosophy, and whose judgment and savvy I trust, what do they think of it?" [53]

This theme of trust as a key component of cue-giving relationships in unitary democracy also emerged in Mansbridge's analysis of an urban crisis center, Helpline. She found that the "less powerful" members of that unitary democracy were unconcerned about the unequal distribution of power, primarily because they believed that they shared common interests with those who had greater power in the organization. She noted that, in the responses these members made during her interviews with them:

The word "trust" appeared over and over...: "There was trust; I respected [her]"; "There's a high level of trust of people in the middle [of the power circle]"; "It seems perfectly natural to me, as long as I trust [them]"; "Those people don't misuse their power ... we trust [them]"; "People feel they can trust [him] and [him]"; "I trust [him] because of his ideals"; "I trust [him]." [54]

Mansbridge contended that these feelings of trust on the part of those with less power in the organization helped to explain why people who believed strongly in political equality nevertheless accepted some degree of inequality in Helpline. Common interests and a trust in those with greater power to act on the basis of those interests removed the need for less powerful members to have their interests protected by political equality.

The element of trust in the legislative cue network works in analogous ways. A recipient's trust in a cue giver, for example, serves to increase the latter's power or influence. Those who hold positions of formal power such as party officer or committee leader are also likely sources of cues for many members. On the other hand, the scope of the intermediary cue network in particular and the fact that cue systems vary with the type of issue under consideration contribute to a diffusion of power within Congress. The pattern of trust evident in the legislative cue network can have unitary significance by making the issue of member equality less important. The cue system provides a continuing basis for members' discovery of common interests. If Fenno is correct in characterizing legislators as inductive thinkers, then a colleague's cue might represent a "concrete, detailed event" in an inductive process, and a member's acceptance "on faith" of that cue's value component might be a step toward a recognition of overlapping interests, empathy, or awareness of a shared principle. That is the kind of information central to the achievement of unitary democracy in Congress.

Summary

Information is a subject of central and recurring importance in both democratic theory and studies of Congress. Discussions of democracy generally focus on the informational requirements of voters and policy makers to meet standards of accountability. In the case of Congress, those standards are applied to its external relationships with constituencies or the executive branch.

The framework of adversary and unitary democracy leads instead to a focus on the internal relationships of Congress. These two models of democracy provide a basis for ordering and understanding Congress's use of information, and they also provide standards for evaluating how different types of information and patterns of information usage relate to congressional democracy. Reforms that increase the volume of information of value in adversary democracy may actually impede the achievement of unitary democracy. Knowing what kinds of information facilitate each type of democracy at each stage of congressional policy making aids in understanding the workings of congressional democracy and in seeing how they can be improved.

NOTES

1. Aage R. Clausen, *How Congressmen Decide: A Policy Focus* (New York: St. Martin's, 1973); John W. Kingdon, *Congressmen's Voting Decisions* (New York: Harper & Row, 1981); Donald R. Matthews and James A. Stimson, *Yeas and Nays: Normal Decision-Making in the U.S. House of Representatives* (New York: Wiley, 1975).
2. Jane J. Mansbridge, *Beyond Adversary Democracy* (Chicago: University of Chicago Press, 1983), 82, 87, and 103.
3. Ibid., 81 and 101.
4. Ibid., 80.
5. Jane J. Mansbridge, "Living with Conflict: Representation in the Theory of Adversary Democracy," *Ethics* 99 (April 1981): 473.

6. Ibid., 473 and 474.
7. Mansbridge, *Beyond Adversary Democracy*, 347-348, nn. 5 and 6.
8. U.S. Senate, *Organization of the Congress*, S. Rept. 1011, 79th Cong., 2nd sess., 9, quoted in James L. Sundquist, *The Decline and Resurgence of Congress* (Washington, D.C.: Brookings Institution, 1981), 402.
9. All of the data in this paragraph were drawn from Norman J. Ornstein et al., *Vital Statistics on Congress, 1982* (Washington, D.C.: American Enterprise Institute, 1982), 105-116.
10. Michael J. Malbin, *Unelected Representatives: Congressional Staff and the Future of Representative Government* (New York: Basic Books, 1980), 239.
11. House Commission on Administrative Review, *Final Report*, H. Doc. 95-272, 95th Cong., 1st sess., 1977, 668.
12. Ibid.
13. Unnamed representative, quoted in Kingdon, *Voting Decisions*, 231-232.
14. Unnamed senator, quoted in Norman J. Ornstein and David Rohde, "Resource Usage, Information, and Policymaking in the Senate," in *Congress and Public Policy: A Source Book of Documents and Readings*, ed. David C. Kozak and John D. Macartney (Homewood, Ill.: Dorsey, 1982), 309-310.
15. Ibid., 310. A related problem—that the more information members receive, the more they realize they do not know—emerges in the lament of Rep. Al Swift, D-Wash.: "I don't know if I have been eating magic mushrooms or wandering around Alice's Wonderland, but the more I learn about this field the bigger it gets. I'm always losing ground. I think I'm going to cry." Quoted in Stephen E. Frantzich, *Computers in Congress: The Politics of Information* (Beverly Hills, Calif.: Sage, 1982), 11.
16. Malbin, *Unelected Representatives*, 239-251.
17. Ibid., 243.
18. Frantzich, *Computers in Congress*, 31. Matthews and Stimson (*Yeas and Nays*, 57, n. 7) make a similar distinction between "cues," which include an evaluative component, and what David Kovenock has called "influential decision premises," which may be purely empirical statements.
19. Edward V. Schneier, Jr., "Legislative Intelligence and the Committee System," in House Select Committee on Committees, *Committee Organization in the House*, H. Doc. 94-187, 93rd Cong., 1st sess., 1973, 2:761.
20. Anthony King, "How to Strengthen Legislatures—Assuming That We Want To," in *The Role of the Legislature in Western Democracies*, ed. Norman J. Ornstein (Washington, D.C.: American Enterprise Institute, 1981), 84. King's "knowledge (of a kind)" corresponds more closely to "data" or "information" than it does to the "knowledge" of Frantzich and Schneier.
21. Arthur W. Macmahon, "Congressional Oversight of Administration: The Power of the Purse," quoted in Roger H. Davidson and David Kovenock, "The Catfish and the Fisherman: Congress and Prescriptive Political Science," *American Behavioral Scientist* 10 (June 1967): 25. A similar argument has been made more recently in Theodore Lowi, *The End of Liberalism* (New York: W. W. Norton, 1979), 305-309.
22. H. Owen Porter, "Legislative Information Needs and Staff Resources in the American States," in *Legislative Staffing: A Comparative Perspective*, ed. James J. Heaphey and Alan P. Balutis (New York: Wiley, 1975), 45-46. Porter's study focused on the Virginia and Michigan legislatures, but the discussion and

conclusions were presented in a generalized and comparative form applicable to studies of the national legislature.

23. Kingdon, *Voting Decisions*, 232.
24. Edward V. Schneier, Jr., statement in *Committee Organization in the House*, 2:326.
25. King, "How to Strengthen Legislatures," 85. For another view of the impact of technical competence on legislatures, see Matthews and Stimson, *Yeas and Nays*, 159-160.
26. Frantzich, *Computers in Congress*, 17-28.
27. For more on stages of policy making, see Charles O. Jones, *An Introduction to the Study of Public Policy* (North Scituate, Mass.: Duxbury Press, 1977); Charles O. Jones, *The United States Congress: People, Place, Policy* (Homewood, Ill.: Dorsey, 1982), 354-378; and David Price, *Who Makes the Laws?* (Cambridge, Mass.: Schenkman, 1972), 4-5. The idea of different information needs at various stages of the process is discussed in Porter, "Legislative Information Needs," and Louis Maisel, "Congressional Information Sources," in *The House at Work*, ed. Joseph Cooper and G. Calvin Mackenzie (Austin: University of Texas Press, 1981).
28. Richard E. Neustadt, *Presidential Power: The Politics of Leadership* (New York: Wiley, 1960), 6-7.
29. Randall B. Ripley and Grace A. Franklin, *Congress, the Bureaucracy, and Public Policy* (Homewood, Ill.: Dorsey, 1980), 218.
30. Michael J. Malbin, "Delegation, Deliberation, and the New Role of Congressional Staff," in *The New Congress*, ed. Thomas E. Mann and Norman J. Ornstein (Washington, D.C.: American Enterprise Institute, 1981), 154.
31. Richard F. Fenno, Jr., remarks in "Discussion," in Ornstein, *Legislature in Western Democracies*, 173.
32. Paul C. Light, "Presidents as Domestic Policymakers," in *Rethinking the Presidency*, ed. Thomas E. Cronin (Boston: Little, Brown, 1982), 367.
33. Martin Tolchin, "Pick a Number, Any Politically Powerful Number," *New York Times*, June 5, 1984, A 24.
34. Malbin, "Delegation," 162-163. Perhaps the classic statement of legislators' distrust of quantitative information is that of the fictional member of Parliament Frank Greystock: "As one of the legislators of the country I am prepared to state that statistics are always false." Anthony Trollope, *The Eustace Diamonds* (1873; reprint, New York: Penguin, 1977), 258.
35. Malbin, "Delegation," 157.
36. Kingdon, *Voting Decisions*, 18-20, and Matthews and Stimson, *Yeas and Nays*, 150-160. A study conducted for the House Commission on Administrative Review found staff to be a more important information source than did either Kingdon or Matthews and Stimson: see its *Final Report* (n. 11 above), 670-674.
37. Charles A. Vanik, "Congress Is Deliberative: Compared to What?" in *The United States Congress: Proceedings of the Thomas P. O'Neill, Jr., Symposium*, ed. Dennis Hale (Chestnut Hill, Mass.: Boston College, 1981), 18.
38. Unnamed representative, quoted in Matthews and Stimson, *Yeas and Nays*, 24.
39. Ibid., 49-51. Cf. the similar discussion in Kingdon, *Voting Decisions*, 73.
40. Malbin, *Unelected Representatives*, 241.

41. Ibid., 241-242.
42. Kingdon, *Voting Decisions*, 232, and Frantzich, *Computers in Congress*, 37.
43. Matthews and Stimson, *Yeas and Nays*, 152.
44. *Congress Off the Record: The Candid Analysis of Seven Members*, ed. John F. Bibby (Washington, D.C.: American Enterprise Institute, 1983), 23-24.
45. Frantzich, *Computers in Congress*, 42, and Harrison W. Fox, Jr., and Susan Webb Hammond, *Congressional Staffs: The Invisible Force in American Lawmaking* (New York: Free Press, 1977), 148.
46. Malbin, "Delegation," 163-177.
47. Frantzich, *Computers in Congress*, 21.
48. Dianne Dumanoski, "Study Says Acid Rain Answer Not in More Research," *Boston Globe*, June 21, 1984, 5.
49. Mansbridge, *Beyond Adversary Democracy*, 27 and 72. Later (297), Mansbridge discusses some specific forms that these common interests can take even in a primarily adversarial system such as that of the United States. These are consensus on the "rules of the game," a unitary response to outside threats, the efficient administration of technical policies by a national bureaucracy, and the anticipated benefits of a changed economic system.
50. Matthews and Stimson, *Yeas and Nays*, 152.
51. Unnamed representative, quoted in Porter, "Legislative Information Needs," 45.
52. House Commission on Administrative Review, *Final Report*, 676.
53. Unnamed representatives, quoted in Matthews and Stimson, *Yeas and Nays*, 48, 61, and 61.
54. Mansbridge, *Beyond Adversary Democracy*, 362, n. 1.

Foreign Policy and the Search for Consensus 7

Assertion of a national interest to guide policy making is perhaps nowhere clearer than in the area of foreign policy. While the concept of national interest can of course be found in policy making in all areas, and while policy making in foreign affairs certainly involves constituency and particularized interests, the relative emphasis given to national interests in foreign policy making serves to distinguish it from other policy areas.

Much attention has been given to the effectiveness of Congress in the realm of foreign policy and, more broadly, to the quality of foreign-policy formulation and implementation by democracies. Once again, the question guiding the present analysis is whether the conceptual framework of adversary and unitary democracy can yield new insights into these problems. The question is investigated in terms of the long-standing dispute between presidents and Congress over the making of foreign policy, the search for consensus, the distinction between policy formulation and implementation, and unitary aspects of congressional behavior in foreign policy.

Congress, the President, and Foreign Policy

From George Washington to Ronald Reagan, presidents have regarded foreign policy as their special province. Presidents as different as

Richard Nixon and John Kennedy have agreed on the importance of the chief executive in the making of foreign policy. Nixon has said: "This country could run itself domestically—without a President. All you need is a competent Cabinet to run the country at home. You need a President for foreign policy; no Secretary of State is really important; the President makes foreign policy." John Kennedy has echoed the thought: "It really is true that foreign affairs is the only important issue for a President to handle." [1] The primacy of foreign policy to presidents is reflected in the time they devote to it. It has been estimated that, in recent administrations, between one-half and two-thirds of the president's time has been devoted to foreign-policy and national-security affairs. [2]

The Constitution, historical precedents, and statutes, however, also give Congress a role in foreign policy. The Senate's power to ratify treaties and congressional control of funding, which naturally includes funding for foreign and military policies, are established by the Constitution. Statutes such as the War Powers Resolution of 1973, the Arms Control Export Act of 1976, and the Nuclear Nonproliferation Act of 1978 all give Congress active and specific foreign-policy responsibilities. Since Congress does, therefore, share policy-making powers in foreign affairs with the executive, the question of the distinction between their responsibilities is raised.

The first week of April 1984 was a time of particularly sharp conflict between the president and Congress over foreign policy. A debate over "who lost Lebanon?" had been intensifying since February, when President Reagan had ordered Marines to move from the Beirut airport to ships offshore. Meanwhile, reports that the United States had mined harbors in Nicaragua and had rejected World Court jurisdiction over the issue produced a storm of criticism from members of Congress, and resolutions were adopted in both chambers condemning the mining. On April 6, President Reagan made a speech about Congress and foreign policy, in which he said:

> The most far-reaching consequence of the past decade's Congressional activism is this: bipartisan consensus-building has become a central responsibility of Congressional leadership as well as of Executive leadership. If we're to have a sustainable foreign policy, the Congress must support the practical details of policy, not just the general goals.
>
> We have demonstrated the capacity for such jointly responsible leadership in certain areas; but we've seen setbacks for bipartisanship, too. I believe that once we established bipartisan agreement on our course in Lebanon, the subsequent second-guessing about whether we ought to keep our men there severely undermined our policy....

> To understand and solve this problem—this problem of joint responsibility—we have to go beyond the familiar questions of who should be stronger, the President or the Congress. The more, basic problem is, in this post-Vietnam era, Congress has not yet developed capacities for coherent, responsible action needed to carry out the new foreign policy powers it has taken for itself.[3]

The congressional role in foreign policy being called for by President Reagan was one of jointly working with the executive branch to build a policy consensus. Once such a consensus had been achieved, Congress would be expected to support the means of implementing the policy (the "practical details") and refrain from further debate on the policy itself. President Reagan's national security adviser, Robert C. McFarlane, was even more specific about the distinction between policy formulation and policy implementation and its implication for the role of Congress. McFarlane said that Congress should be encouraged to debate and disagree with the president in the "formation" of policy, but, he warned, "Once that policy is formed, it can seriously undermine its hope of success if there is a continuing repetition of this earlier disagreement." He went so far as to suggest that members of Congress critical of an established policy should express that criticism privately and in writing to the president rather than in an open forum.[4]

Opponents argued that the position outlined by the president and his national security adviser amounted to an attempt to limit criticism. House majority leader Jim Wright, D-Texas, for example, said that Reagan's speech showed that the president "expects Congress to be a silent partner, to put up the money and keep its mouth shut and accept the blame whenever anything goes wrong."[5] Speaker O'Neill pointed out that Reagan himself had engaged in partisan criticism of the foreign policy of previous administrations rather than serving as a bipartisan supporter of such policy.[6] Democratic leaders in general believed at the time that criticism of Reagan's foreign policy would be their strongest suit in the 1984 campaign.

To dismiss the president's position as mere campaign rhetoric or as an attempt to limit debate, however, is to overlook the fact that it can also be found in political science literature on the subject. For example, Stephen Krasner has suggested that "the President and those bureaus relatively insulated from societal pressures, which are the only institutions capable of formulating the national interest ... must always struggle against an inherent tendency for power and control to be dissipated and dispersed," and that Congress is a primary source of this dispersion, because it "offer[s] many points of access for societal groups."⁷ Crabb and Holt have expressed the belief that the problem may be becoming more severe:

> By the early 1980s Congress appeared to be more decentralized, fragmented, and resistant to unifying influences than in any previous period of American history. To date Congress has supplied little evidence to show that it is prepared to adapt its own organizational structure and internal procedures to the demands of the active foreign policy role its members are determined to play.⁸

Members of Congress have made similar observations. Sen. Barry Goldwater, R-Ariz., said in 1976 that a president "who would not be disturbed by the politics of the moment, would use these powers far more wisely in the long run of history than a Congress which is constantly looking toward the political results." The senior Republican on the House Foreign Affairs Committee, William S. Broomfield of Michigan, said at about the same time that he was "disturbed when I sensed that individual legislators might assess a foreign policy issue not by the standards of the national interest, but by what is right politically or will look good in the district." These statements were made by Republicans during a Republican administration and so might be suspected of having partisan motivation, but Democrats have also put forward the same ideas. Rep. Lee H. Hamilton, D-Ind., the principal author of a 1984 resolution drafted by House Democrats that criticized U.S. policy in Lebanon, has written: "Diplomacy requires a long view of the national interest. Congress is influenced by short-term interests. Its members are parochial and overly concerned with reelection." Another Democratic activist on foreign policy, Sen. Adlai Stevenson III, D-Ill., in the course of a speech in 1976 excoriating the foreign policy of the Ford administration, conceded that "Congress is poorly suited for a major role in the formulation and implementation of foreign policy."⁹

In sum, many of the characteristics that differentiate Congress from the executive and that have been discussed previously (see chapter 3) also affect Congress's conduct in the making of foreign policy. These include the focus on reelection, narrow constituencies, decentralized structure, delay in decision making, limited information, tendency to favor short-run solutions, susceptibility to political pressure, and the absence of a comprehensive view of the national interest. Those who take the "presidential" position in foreign policy, however, not only believe that Congress should not involve itself in operational matters once a foreign-policy consensus has been achieved, but also assume that such a consensus is possible in the first place. How plausible is that assumption?

Consensus _____

The idea of consensus is one that appears regularly in discussions of foreign policy, though not always with the same meaning. Sundquist has observed: "When the country lost its faith in the wisdom of the Vietnam War, the postwar national consensus on foreign policy disintegrated. For the consensus had been built on the broad strategic objective of containing communist expansion, and Vietnam had been only the logical and latest extension of that policy." Destler, however, saw Vietnam not as the end of an old consensus but as the beginning of a new one:

> If a viewpoint becomes widely shared and persists over a period of years, it can become particularly influential. A dramatic example is the consensus that developed against the Vietnam War, a consensus that not only produced the War Powers Resolution and the Indochina bombing ban, but also led to a subsequent prohibition against U.S. involvement in the Angolan civil war.

Brenner, like Sundquist, described the foreign-policy consensus that emerged from World War II as a casualty of Vietnam, and he saw much of the subsequent executive-legislative interaction in foreign policy as a battle over who would define the new consensus:

> The shaping of the new consensus was up for grabs, and legislators believed that they could and should have a strong hand in the task. Members were trying to establish a new foreign-policy consensus, rooted in principles of human rights and respect for each country's sovereignty, when they restricted the executive's freedom to intervene in Angola, to support repressive regimes in the Third World, and to be an arms merchant to the world. . . . Of course, the executive branch also sought to establish its version of the new consensus. Under President Carter the executive position became a reversion to dogmatic anti-Sovietism.[10]

Other analysts, as well as political leaders, tend to use consensus in a narrower, institutional sense when discussing the making of foreign policy. Representative Hamilton, recognized by colleagues as a leader in this area, recently observed that "the toughest thing to do in this institution is to build consensus." Columnist Anthony Lewis wrote that a little-noticed but important development of the early stages of the 1984 presidential campaign was "the emergence of a Democratic consensus on foreign policy." And Senate minority leader Robert C. Byrd, in explaining the cohesive Democratic vote against a 1983 resolution keeping the Marines in Lebanon, said: "The consensus that is evident from our votes on this issue is a consensus of conscience."[11]

Despite the different meanings they gave to consensus, all of these observers regarded it as a positive value and a necessity in the making of foreign policy. Not everyone, however, shares even these views. Gelb and Betts, for example, concluded from their analysis of the Vietnam War that consensus on a broad foreign-policy doctrine can have the effect of precluding consideration of alternative policies and of producing operational rigidity.[12] Chace has argued that the increased complexity of international political, economic, and military relations has made consensus impossible and that it "may no longer be possible to resurrect [a consensus] short of war." Political leaders, he said, "may simply have to learn to conduct foreign policy for a very long time without a single unifying theme on which to base a broad national consensus."[13] Alexander George, in his book on decision making in foreign policy, has written about the detrimental effects of "spontaneous consensus" and "illusory consensus."[14]

Consensus may take on additional positive or negative value when it is used for tactical reasons in political debate. If members of Congress accepted the contention that President Reagan put forth in his April 1984 speech—that a bipartisan consensus existed on U.S. policy in Lebanon—then they would be more likely to accept his admonition to support the "practical details" as well as the "general goals" of that policy. The idea of consensus can thus have practical effects; it can be used as a way of structuring debate and influencing policy as well as a tool for analysis.[15] The post-Vietnam struggle between Congress and the president to define a new consensus reflects an attempt by both sides to establish the context of foreign policy. How people regard consensus, in other words, depends not only on the meaning given to the term but also on how the concept is being used in the political context in which it is invoked.

Democracy and a coherent foreign policy have sometimes been presented as being mutually exclusive. Destler, for example, has written that a "political-procedural dilemma" underlies the conflict between the president and Congress in this area. "Americans want two things that often prove incompatible in practice: *democratic government* (involving on-going competition among a range of U.S. interests and perspectives) and *effective foreign policy* (which requires settling on specific goals and pursuing them consistently)."[16] The process of "settling on specific goals and pursuing them consistently" is that of making foreign policy by consensus. The type of democracy presented as being inconsistent with that process is easily recognizable as adversary democracy, as indicated by reference to "ongoing competition" among a range of interests and perspectives.

Unitary democracy, however, operates by consensus. Deliberation among decision makers leads them either to create common ground or to recognize existing common interests. Mansbridge describes decision making by consensus as "a form of decision making in which, after discussion, one or more members of the assembly sum up prevailing sentiment, and if no objections are voiced, this becomes agreed-on policy." She also notes that it is not the formal procedure that is important to an understanding of consensus, for legislatures can engage in consensual decision making even while following formal majoritarian procedures. Rather, the essence of consensual decision making is arriving at the "prevailing sentiment." [17]

Adversary democracy may indeed be incompatible with a foreign policy based on consistent pursuit of shared goals, but unitary democracy need not be. The implications of this should be clear. A legislature that is exclusively adversarial can only work against development of a foreign-policy consensus. If it is to play a part in building consensus instead, a legislature (and a president as well) must act, at least some of the time, along the lines of unitary democracy. What are the bases on which Congress might do this?

At least three different meanings of consensus emerge in discussions of the making of foreign policy: widespread agreement on fundamental values, on policies designed to maximize those values, and on the process for developing those policies. Political actors who join in a consensus on one level do not necessarily do so on other levels. They may agree on goals or ends but disagree on means, on the best way to achieve those goals. But since the process of consensus-building often consists of creating agreement on one level on the basis of an existing agreement on another, it is helpful to recognize these different levels of agreement and the corresponding forms of consensus.

Value Consensus

George identifies three fundamental values that have served as the basis of American foreign policy for some time. Although there has been widespread disagreement over their relative importance (as well as, of course, over the substance of foreign policy), all parties have acknowledged the preeminence of these three values. These "irreducible national interests," as George calls them, are physical survival, liberty, and economic subsistence. By physical survival, George means the survival of a country's citizens, not necessarily the preservation of territorial borders or sovereign independence. Liberty is the ability of citizens to choose their own form of government and the existence of a nonarbitrary system of laws. The economic value, like the others, is expressed as a minimum condition. While George recognizes that governments generally seek to maximize economic welfare, he also points out that the pursuit of liberty or physical survival may require a reduction in economic standards. Subsistence represents the irreducible national interest in the economic sphere. It is an interest governments pursue even in wartime.[18]

The concept of national interest or interests has been criticized and even dismissed by some political analysts, especially when the concept is advanced as a way to guide policy making. Chace, for example, has remarked that those who seek to use the concept of national interest for that purpose "usually end up dodging all the hard questions that surround such situations as the Middle East or southern Africa, not to mention bilateral relations with the Soviet Union. In every case, there are elements of the 'national interest' on both sides of any difficult decision; too often those who invoke the phrase are trying to load the dice in favor of the outcome they think most important." [19] The essence of this criticism is that the concept of national interest is of little help to decision makers who must make choices among values. George's formulation of irreducible national interests is designed to overcome that problem by its minimalist approach. The interests of physical survival, liberty, and economic subsistence, he argues, take priority over any other interests of the state, and there is no hierarchy of importance among them. That is, a consensus exists among makers of foreign policy not only on the primacy of these three values over all others, but also on the need to *avoid* having to rank them relative to each other. A successful foreign policy is one that never requires decision makers to decide whether physical survival is more important than liberty or economic subsistence.

Policy Consensus

It is relatively easy to achieve widespread agreement on goals when no action is required. Policy, however, is a course of action taken to achieve particular goals. Since policy requires commitment of limited resources, it also involves choosing among different courses of action and different goals. Consensus on policy is therefore less likely to occur than consensus on basic values, except perhaps, to the degree that policy makers perceive a threat to the "irreducible national interests."

As noted above, a foreign-policy consensus guided American policy makers from the end of World War II until the late 1960s. That consensus revolved around a policy of containment: On the basis of the belief that international Communism represented a threat to the West's vital interests of survival and liberty, it was proposed that—as articulated in George Kennan's classic 1947 article in *Foreign Affairs*—the Soviet Union's, and later China's, tendencies toward expansion be checked by a major commitment of economic and military resources, while avoiding a nuclear war. American involvement in Vietnam was an expression of this policy of containment. Congressional questioning of whether U.S. national interests were actually at stake in Vietnam eventually led to a breakdown of that consensus, but not to a complete abandonment of the policy of containment, which continues to enjoy wide support in both the executive and the legislative branches, despite occasional reports of the policy's demise. When, for example, President Reagan appealed for congressional approval of increased military aid for El Salvador in May 1984, he declared: "If we do nothing or if we continue to provide too little help, our choice will be a Communist Central America with additional Communist military bases on the mainland of this hemisphere, and Communist subversion spreading southward and northward." [20] The House passed the aid bill by a margin of only four votes, which indicates that the consensus is no longer widely shared—but the fact that it passed at all suggests that containment is still an important policy for many in Congress as well as in the executive branch.

Attempts have been made in the last decade to forge a new policy consensus that would serve in much the same way as containment did for 25 years after the end of World War II. In 1972 and 1973, for example, the Nixon administration put forward the principle of detente as the overarching foreign policy of the United States. In 1977, the Carter administration said that advancement of human rights would be the guiding force of U.S. foreign policy. Neither of these has won consensus to the extent that containment had. Detente was abandoned even by the administration that introduced it when Soviet actions in the Middle East, Africa, and Latin America were perceived as threats to U.S. interests, and although Congress has gone beyond several administrations in applying the human-rights principle to foreign policies, disagreements over both the substance and the standards of human rights continue to divide Congress and the president.

It is the absence of consensus at the policy level more than at any other level that has attracted the attention of analysts. Their study of

U.S. policy toward Vietnam led Gelb and Betts to suggest that avoiding commitment to a broad foreign-policy doctrine such as containment would bring needed flexibility to the making of U.S. foreign policy. Chace, as has been noted, has said that the complexity of international relations today made a consensus on foreign policy impossible in any case. Crabb and Holt have put forward the idea that lack of a foreign-policy consensus over the last decade and a half has given Congress both "an opportunity and an incentive" for a more active role in the formulation of foreign policy. A gathering of foreign-policy conservatives under the auspices of the Committee for the Free World, in May 1984, criticized the Reagan administration for its failure to "rally a consensus" for a foreign policy of "containment plus." [21]

Procedural Consensus

Foreign-policy decisions often come down to a question of whether a nation will use force to pursue its objectives. George's "irreducible national interests" represent the minimal values a nation is willing to protect by use of force, but a central issue in foreign policy is the identification of the other values that a nation is prepared to defend in the same way.[22] A policy consensus, such as that on containment, provides standards for dealing with that issue, and it thereby gives a consistency to foreign policy. While Congress rejected containment as the basis of foreign policy in the 1970s, it neither went back to the prewar philosophy of isolationism nor put forth an alternative organizing principle. Sundquist has described the result:

> With such simple goals as involvement nowhere and involvement everywhere eliminated, that left only the in-between option—a policy of involvement on occasion, at some time, in some places. But there was no simple and reliable principle to decide the when and the where. That left Congress free to act in individual cases as its mood might dictate, without the constraints imposed by broader policy considerations. It could let feelings and emotions, even impulse—and the constituent pressures behind them—be the guide.[23]

George also addressed this problem: "Where questions of trade-offs at the margin among scores, or hundreds, of different interests and values are involved, specifying unambiguous criteria for choice will be a hopeless task." Yet George also warned of the dangerous consequences "if no standards, and no consistent procedures, are applied to determine what interests are to be pursued, and with what means." He concluded: "One way out of this dilemma would be to specify a set of procedures, or decision-rules,' that policymakers would need to follow in order to assure the legitimacy of their actions." [24]

In other words, in the absence of a consensus on values, a consensus on procedure might give the necessary standards and consistency to the making of foreign policy. Sundquist observed that the "new approach" to foreign policy announced by President Nixon in 1970 hinted at such a procedural focus, but the administration failed to specify what the new procedure would be.[25] The many congressional reforms of the 1970s, which have served as the basis of that institution's new activism in foreign policy, also had a procedural focus. The War Powers Resolution of 1973, for example, set forth an elaborate set of procedures which both the president and Congress must follow in making decisions about the use of U.S. troops abroad. Reforms in the Foreign Assistance Act in 1976 and the International Security Assistance Act in 1978 established procedures by which the executive branch was to report to Congress on human rights practices in recipient nations before military assistance could be provided.

A procedural consensus, or agreement on the "rules of the game," can exist in even the most factious adversary democracy. A commitment to abide by majority rule, for example, is a requirement of adversary democracy. But if procedural consensus allows deliberation to take place, it can also point the deliberative body in the direction of a broader consensus, one that encompasses some policies as well as procedures, and in that sense many of the congressional reforms in the making of foreign policy might be linked with unitary democracy.

One benefit of distinguishing among value, policy, and procedural consensuses is that it helps us realize that strong foreign-policy disagreements between the president and Congress can exist at the same time as there is general agreement between the two branches. That, in turn, leads us to avoid absolute statements regarding the presence or absence of consensus and to appreciate the several levels on which consensus-building takes place. The distinction also provides a focus of research and a basis of evaluation in considering the effects of congressional reforms on the making of foreign policy.

Policy Formulation and Implementation

The idea that Congress may have a hand in formulating foreign policy but the executive is responsible for implementing it is another concept often found in discussions of the making of foreign policy. "The special responsibility of the Congress," Representative Hamilton has written, "is to provide informed consent on the substance of foreign policy. The legislative pace simply does not lend itself to supervision of the day-to-day conduct of foreign policy." Destler has put the same thought in more pointed form: "The genius of Congress is democracy, diversity, debate. Often Congress nurtures creativity. . . . The executive, by contrast, offers the hierarchy and concentrated formal authority that make coherent policy execution at least possible." Brenner refers to the "old prescription" which asserts "that Congress is best suited to formulate foreign policy equally with the executive and should remove itself from independent execution of policy." [26]

Nevertheless, Congress has, at times, not been content with having a voice in the formulation of foreign policy but has also sought control over its implementation. Sundquist cited four instances that characterized the "new congressional ascendancy" in foreign policy: ending the Vietnam war; the 1974 Jackson-Vanik amendment, linking trade with the Soviet Union to Jewish emigration; the 1974 embargo on military aid to Turkey; and the 1975 cutoff of funds for covert aid in Angola. He argued that these actions demonstrated an attempt by Congress to "take command" of foreign policy, "to reverse the presidential policy in a series of operational decisions." [27]

Indeed, the distinction between policy formulation and implementation is not as easy to maintain as it might seem at first glance. Jones has pointed out that formulation "is a derivative of 'formula' and means simply to develop a plan, a method, a prescription—in this case for alleviating some need, for acting on a problem." [28] Formulation is the first stage in the policy-development process. Implementation comes later and consists of activities directed toward putting a policy into effect, a "conscious conversion of policy plans into reality." [29] There are three particular types of activities that make up policy implementation: (1) interpreting policy and converting policy goals into specific directives; (2) organizing the governmental units responsible for carrying out those directives; and (3) providing resources to those units so that they can act.[30] But sometimes implementation of necessity becomes an extension of formulation. As Jones has said, the formulation stage frequently leaves "unresolved dilemmas . . . making implementation a dynamic concept involving continuing efforts to discern what should and can be accomplished." [31]

It is this dynamic aspect of implementation which makes the distinction between formulation and implementation difficult to maintain. There is no fixed point at which formulation is complete and implementation begins. The execution of a policy can lead to reformulation of the problem to be solved, the goals to be achieved, and the means available for achieving them. This characteristic complicates greatly, or even undercuts, the distinction used so often in describing the congressional role in foreign policy.

Consider, for example, the case of U.S. policy toward Lebanon, which was mentioned earlier. In September 1983, under the procedures established by the War Powers Resolution of 1973, Congress passed a resolution that authorized the president to keep a force of Marines in Beirut for 18 months, prohibited an expansion of that force without congressional approval, and authorized the president to use "such protective measures as may be necessary to ensure the safety of the Multinational Force in Lebanon." [32] On February 7, 1984, President Reagan announced that the 1,600 Marines in Lebanon would be moved from Beirut to U.S. ships in the area, and he also ordered an intensified shelling of areas of Lebanon by U.S. naval forces. On February 8, 1984, the guns of the battleship New Jersey bombarded hills around Beirut for nine hours. The administration spokesman, Larry Speakes, said on that day that the shelling was intended to support the government of Lebanon, but on the next day he said it was carried out to protect the Marines. Some members of Congress, including Speaker O'Neill, argued that the shelling was in violation of the September resolution of Congress because it was not a "protective measure." The statement of policy in the resolution said that U.S. forces were to perform a neutral peacekeeping function. In a televised address on October 27, however, President Reagan had said the U.S. presence in Lebanon was needed to protect the nation's "vital interests" in the area and to support the Lebanese government.[33] The intensive shelling in February might be in accordance with those policies but not with the neutral peacekeeping and limited protective policies of the congressional resolution. Thus, although the debate between Congress and the president that took place early in 1984 seemed to center on policy implementation (the role of the Marines and the February shelling), it was clearly a case in which the implementation of a policy was affecting the substance of the policy itself. To deny a congressional role in implementation would be to deny Congress a role in making that policy.

The connection between the congressional role in foreign policy and the implementation of that policy in another sense of the term is illustrated in an analysis by Destler of the withdrawal of the SALT II treaty by the Carter administration in 1980 and the successful conclusion of the multilateral trade negotiations the previous year. Destler sought to determine why it was that on trade, "unlike on SALT, the executive and legislative branches were able to arrive at a common outcome, a consistent U.S. foreign policy stance." [34] He concluded that one reason for the difference had to do with the nature of the congressional process:

> On trade, congressional attention focused not on the text of the codes themselves but on a separate product—the implementation legislation. This needed to be consistent with the Geneva package, and foreign governments sought to influence it. But it did not have to be negotiated—or renegotiated—with them. This gave legislators a vehicle for making an impact on policy without threatening to undo the international accord. [35]

SALT II, by contrast, did not provide such a separation between the treaty and the implementing legislation. Some senators attempted to convert the defense budget into de facto implementing legislation, for SALT II, but they were unable to do so. One lesson from this comparison is that an active congressional role in shaping implementation can help to produce legislative-executive accord in the formulation of foreign policy.

Problems and Changes in the Congressional Role

The recent debates between the president and Congress over procedures and proper executive and legislative roles in the determination of foreign policy are indicative of changes in the foreign-policy process. Franck and Weisband have said that "an entire system of power has been overturned" since the end of the Vietnam War—a change of sufficient magnitude to warrant calling it a revolution:

> Among the booty redistributed by the revolution was control over U.S. foreign policy, long a Presidential perquisite. With the revolution came those questions characteristic of radical breaks with an established order. Can the revolutionaries get organized or will they be themselves devoured, victims of disordered revolutionary energy? Having seized power, can they couple it with purpose? Can they protect the national interest from enemies seeking to take advantage of the upheaval? [36]

Other scholars, though they may not use the term "revolution," have raised similar questions about congressional activism in foreign policy. Whether this activism proves to be a fundamental change or simply part of a cyclical pattern depends on the answers given to these questions and on the standards employed for evaluating congressional performance in this area.

Three such standards are implicit in the above passage from the work by Franck and Weisband: effectiveness of organization, agreement on goals or purposes to guide action, and protection of the national interest. Crabb and Holt have proposed similar standards:

> If the House and Senate have now established—and can be expected to maintain—an influential congressional presence in the foreign policy field, how well are they equipped to continue to play this role? Recent experience indicates that the answer must be: rather poorly and inadequately. To date, in terms of organizational, procedural, and behavioral changes required, few members of Congress have faced up squarely to the necessary implications of their demand for a position of equal partnership with the White House in foreign affairs.[37]

The authors go on to say that, to the extent that Congress is "decentralized, fragmented, and resistant to unifying influences," its foreign-policy performance will be regarded negatively.[38]

Standards for measuring congressional activity in foreign policy are derived, naturally enough, from a view of what constitutes effective foreign policy. Destler's suggestion that there is a conflict between an effective foreign policy and the demands of a democratic political system was noted above. Others have expressed the same concern. For example, Spanier and Uslaner also point to the "dilemma" created by the "intrinsic authoritarian necessities of foreign affairs and the democratic needs of the internal order." [39] Crabb and Holt observe that there is general agreement among policy makers "that continuing discord, disunity, and competing efforts within the American government— regardless of whether they arise within the executive branch, within Congress, or from conflicts between the executive and legislative branches—nearly always impair the ability of the United States to achieve its diplomatic objectives." [40]

If the process that produces an "effective foreign policy" or increases the ability to achieve "diplomatic objectives" has certain required characteristics, and the defining characteristics of democracy are just the opposite, then the conflict between democracy and effective foreign policy is inevitable, and the more democratic Congress is, the less suited will it seem for an active role in making foreign policy. In fact, the shortcomings of Congress most often commented upon by those evaluating the institution's performance in foreign policy are precisely those attributed to any democratic political system. Waltz, for example, has noted that criticisms of the ability of democracies to conduct foreign policy have centered on three points. First, because policies in a democracy are based on a shifting majority, they are likely to lack continuity. New elections and new coalitions will produce new policies. Second, when foreign policies become an issue in election campaigns, chances increase that they will be determined by internal pressures as much as by demands of the international environment. Third, steady administration of policy is hindered by occasional arousal of public opinion on a particular matter or by legislative intervention.[41]

Waltz, however, counters these criticisms at least in part by employing a concept of democracy that is different from the purely adversary model implicit in most of them. Although Waltz himself does not use the terms "adversary" and "unitary" democracy, some of the characteristics of democracy that he discusses are, in effect, those of unitary democracy.

Addressing the problem that shifting majorities make for instability and discontinuity in democratic foreign policy, Waltz points out that in the American political system, a number of factors—the absence of party discipline, the system of checks and balances, and such constitutional requirements as the two-thirds vote needed for Senate approval of treaties—effectively require that policies be based on more than a simple majority. "With a wider consensus required, there is less tendency for the next government to undo what the present government has accomplished." [42] Thus, a foreign policy developed in a democratic political system that requires broad consensus rather than a simple majority— which is to say, one that is more unitary—is more likely to be stable. Instability and discontinuity in foreign policy, in other words, are not associated with democracy per se but with a particular type of democracy.

The second criticism, that internal pressures have important effects upon a democracy's foreign policy, is based on the premise of conflicting interests that, again, marks the concept of adversary democracy. There certainly have been cases when internal pressures had major consequences for U.S. foreign policy. Stern found this to be true of the 1974 Jackson-Vanik amendment,[43] and Sundquist and others have seen it in congressional action to cut off military aid to Turkey in 1975. (One member of the House is said to have commented, facetiously but tellingly, that "there are more Greek restaurants in my district than there are Turkish baths.") [44] But there are also cases that demonstrate the influence of national interests on congressional behavior. Schneider's analysis of roll-call votes in the 1970s uncovered consistent patterns of congressional votes on foreign-policy issues, patterns that reflected ideology and perceptions of national interests, whereas there were few of the cleavages one would find if domestic concerns and constituency interests were determining these votes.[45] Brenner's study of congressional initiatives in the early 1970s to normalize relations with Cuba also found that perceived national interests were important determinants of behavior. Even though some members sought to relate their actions toward Cuba to constituency interests such as rice markets or air-conditioner parts, Brenner concluded his study with this observation: "Members act on what they perceive to be national interests and they attempt to fashion policy in accordance with national interests. They support national interests most easily when free from constituency pressure, and in doing so see the national interest ideologically." [46]

The third criticism, that steady administration of policy is difficult to achieve in a democratic system, is once again associated with adversary democracy. It has already been pointed out that it is difficult to separate administration of policy from formulation of policy. When it is also recognized that interruptions in the steady administration of policy are likely to stem from disagreement over the policy itself, it appears that this third criticism is nothing more than a restatement of the first two. It is not the interruptions that are viewed negatively so much as the discontinuity in policy they cause and the internal pressures they are said to reflect. A unitary democratic process that minimizes those factors would also minimize the third criticism.

What this review suggests is that appraisals of the making of foreign policy in a democratic system, and especially of the role of Congress, are often based on an assumption of adversary democracy. Consideration of unitary democracy sheds new light on the problem. Democratic government and an effective foreign policy need not be incompatible in practice.

When the making of foreign policy is viewed from the perspective of adversary democracy, the central question, as stated by Waltz, is apt to be: "In a competition of particular interests, how can it be expected that the common interest will triumph?" [47] When it does triumph (and Waltz cites many instances when it did), political analysts are likely to regard the episodes as deviant cases, aberrations from the normal pattern. The framework of unitary democracy, however, produces a different set of expectations, in which perceptions of national interest are as important as, or more important than, particular interests in determining foreign policy and the role of Congress in making it. The central question that emerges from this perspective is: What is the nature of the consensus or the common interest on which Congress has developed a particular foreign policy? When political analysts look at cases such as the Jackson-Vanik amendment or the Turkish arms embargo from the perspective of unitary democracy, they discover congressional agreement on giving substance to such concepts as freedom of emigration, free speech, and the peaceful settlement of territorial disputes. Explanations of policy must include these unitary forces as well as the adversary, particularistic ones such as the influence of Greek and Jewish constituents.

In fact, the congressional record in foreign policy includes a number of cases in which unitary explanations seem to serve better than adversary ones. The congressional role in establishing human rights as a priority of U.S. foreign policy is one example. Congress seized the initiative in 1973, when it set forth recognition of human rights as a criterion for determining the amount of aid to be given to a foreign nation. Although policy makers continue to differ over the substance and measurement of human rights, they are recognized by all parties as important elements of foreign policy. By all accounts, it is a common interest that was developed in the legislative branch of government. In this effort, Franck and Weisband have said, "Congress was stubbornly opposed by the Nixon and Ford Administrations. . . . Nevertheless, the human rights campaign succeeded beyond all expectations of its congressional sponsors. It was enthusiastically embraced by the new Carter Administration when it took office in 1977." [48] Crabb and Holt are even more emphatic, saying that in its insistence on giving greater weight to human-rights issues, Congress was not only "well ahead of the Nixon and Ford administrations" but "at times . . . even outran Jimmy Carter. . . ." [49]

Congressional action on the Panama Canal treaties provides another illustration of the importance of common interests. According to Franck and Weisband, "During the spring and summer of 1978, sixty-eight Senators had approved a Panama Canal Treaty in a vote that was clearly not motivated by political self-interest." Sundquist has offered a similar conclusion: "The Senate went against powerful constituency pressures to give Carter the benefit of the doubt on the Panama Canal treaties." [50] And on the same subject, Crabb and Holt comment that

> perhaps no episode from recent American diplomatic experience more forcefully communicates Congress's determination to appear as the defender of the nation's diplomatic and security interests. . . . Most senators came to feel that the national interest required ratification of the treaties, unpopular though they might have been. The Senate then proceeded to reduce the issue by prolonged debate and by amending the treaties. Owing to changes made to them on Capitol Hill, the new Panama Canal treaties were successfully presented to the American people as consonant with the security demands of the United States. Without that assurance, it is doubtful that the new treaties could have been ratified. [51]

Agreement on the values expressed in human-rights policies has not precluded disagreement and debate over the substance of human rights or the priority to be given them in the face of competing values such as sovereignty or national security. The consensus reflected in the Panama Canal treaties case is a policy consensus, but certainly not one of the scope of the consensus on containment. Since the demise of the latter, the United States has had no policy consensus to rival it. If there is any consensus that can now serve to unite policy makers, it is a procedural consensus.

An active congressional role in the deployment of military forces is now mandated by the War Powers Resolution of 1973, and similar procedures have been established in legislation governing arms sales, nuclear exports, and intelligence operations, among other areas. Members of Congress may disagree with one another and with executive policy makers over the substance of policy, but there is widespread agreement on the procedures to be followed in the development of policy. A procedural consensus may be regarded as a step toward the building of a policy consensus. This is what Franck and Weisband may have had in mind when they concluded, after reviewing the recent procedural changes:

> Democratic legitimization achieved in this fashion has begun to build a replacement for the national foreign policy consensus shattered by the Vietnam War. The new consensus, however, is characterized by wide participation, painstaking consultation, and hard-fought compromise, whereas the old, too often, was played out as a game of follow the leader.[52]

Summary

Many observers have assigned Congress a secondary role in the making of foreign policy and have pointed to the weaknesses of democracies in formulating and conducting foreign policy. But these positions may owe as much to definition as to observation. To define policy implementation as something distinct from policy formulation, and to give Congress a role only in the latter, effectively removes the institution from the making of foreign policy. In the same way, to recognize national interest as a guide for foreign policy and the presidency as the only institution in American politics capable of recognizing and acting on that interest weakens legislators' claims to a foreign-policy role. Lastly, to argue that democratic processes must exhibit particular characteristics, and then to declare that those characteristics are incompatible with an effective foreign policy, leads to the inevitable conclusion that a democracy cannot produce successful foreign policies.

But the model of democracy implicit in most analyses of the congressional role in foreign policy is that of adversary democracy. Many of the descriptions and conclusions about this role seem less compelling when considered from the perspective of unitary democracy. The ability of Congress to develop a consensus and a shared perception of national interest is a function of unitary processes within the institution. What an adversarial body cannot do might be done by one that is unitary. Congress is both. To fully appreciate both the past behavior of Congress and its potential as a maker of foreign policy, its unitary as well as its adversary characteristics must be considered.

NOTES

1. Nixon quoted in Theodore H. White, *The Making of the President 1968* (New York: Atheneum, 1969), 147; Kennedy quoted in Richard M. Nixon, *RN: Memoirs of Richard Nixon* (New York: Grosset & Dunlap, 1978), 235.
2. Thomas E. Cronin, *The State of the Presidency* (Boston: Little, Brown, 1980), 146. The estimate is based on interviews with presidential aides.
3. *Congressional Quarterly Weekly Report*, April 14, 1984, 870.
4. Steven R. Weisman, "President vs. Congress: Reagan's Confrontational Speech May Put Foreign Policy Issues in Greater Jeopardy," *New York Times*, April 7, 1984, 6.
5. Quoted in John Felton, "Hill Presses Reagan on Central America Policy," *Congressional Quarterly Weekly Report*, April 14, 1984, 832.
6. Diane Granat, "Congress Adjourns for Easter after Foreign Policy Bickering," *Congressional Quarterly Weekly Report*, April 14, 1984, 824.
7. Stephen D. Krasner, *Defending the National Interest: Raw Materials Investment and U.S. Foreign Policy* (Princeton, N.J.: Princeton University Press, 1978), 62-63.
8. Cecil V. Crabb, Jr., and Pat M. Holt, *Invitation to Struggle: Congress, the President, and Foreign Policy*, 2nd ed. (Washington, D.C.: CQ Press, 1984), 243-244.
9. Senator Goldwater, Representative Broomfield, and Senator Stevenson quoted in James L. Sundquist, *The Decline and Resurgence of Congress* (Washington, D.C.: Brookings Institution, 1981), 291; and Lee H. Hamilton, "Congress and Foreign Policy," *Presidential Studies Quarterly* 12 (Spring 1982): 135.
10. Sundquist, *Decline and Resurgence*, 273; I. M. Destler, "Executive-Congressional Conflict in Foreign Policy; Explaining It, Coping with It," in *Congress Reconsidered*, ed. Lawrence C. Dodd and Bruce I. Oppenheimer (Washington, D.C.: CQ Press, 1981), 300; and Philip Brenner, *The Limits and Possibilities of Congress* (New York: St. Martin's, 1983), 93.
11. Representative Hamilton quoted in Martin Tolchin, "How to Win Friends and Influence Foreign Policy," *New York Times*, February 19, 1984, E4;

Anthony Lewis, "Democrats United," ibid., February 23, 1984, A23; and Senator Byrd quoted in David Rogers, "Congress Gives Reagan Authority for Lebanon Force," *Boston Globe*, September 30, 1983, 1.

12. Leslie H. Gelb and Richard K. Betts, *The Irony of Vietnam: The System Worked* (Washington, D.C.: Brookings Institution, 1979), 362-369.

13. James Chace, "Is a Foreign Policy Consensus Possible?" *Foreign Affairs* 57 (Fall 1978): 15 and 16.

14. Alexander George, *Presidential Decisionmaking in Foreign Policy: The Effective Use of Information and Advice* (Boulder, Colo.: Westview, 1980), 122-123 and 132-133.

15. William H. Riker calls this art of manipulating the structure of tastes and alternatives within which decisions are made "heresthetics," and he provides an analysis of it in "Political Theory and the Art of Heresthetics," in *Political Science: The State of the Discipline*, ed. Ada W. Finifter (Washington, D.C.: American Political Science Association, 1983), 47-67.

16. Destler, "Executive-Congressional Conflict," 298.

17. Jane J. Mansbridge, *Beyond Adversary Democracy* (Chicago: University of Chicago Press, 1983), 32.

18. George, *Presidential Decisionmaking*, 223-227.

19. Chace, "Foreign Policy Consensus," 15.

20. Quoted in John Felton, "Reagan Wins Victory on Central America Plan," *Congressional Quarterly Weekly Report*, May 12, 1984, 1086.

21. Gelb and Betts, *Irony of Vietnam*, 362-369; Chace, "Foreign Policy Consensus," 15-16; Crabb and Holt, *Invitation to Struggle*, 62; and Walter Goodman, "Neoconservatives Assess Political Trends and Foreign Policy," *New York Times*, May 14, 1984, B9. Goodman noted that the meeting did not produce any clear idea of what the "plus" was in "containment plus."

22. The term "vital interests" is sometimes used to refer to those interests for which a nation is willing to go to war. President Reagan provoked strong congressional reaction when he stated, on October 24, 1983: "Many Americans are wondering why we must keep our forces in Lebanon. The reason is quite clear. We have vital interests in Lebanon, and our actions are in the cause of world peace." This was the first assertion of "vital interests" in the area and was seen by many members of Congress as an unjustified escalation of the stakes there. See Richard Whittle, "Lebanon: Defining the U.S. 'Vital Interest,'" *Congressional Quarterly Weekly Report*, October 29, 1983, 2219-2220.

23. Sundquist, *Decline and Resurgence*, 275.

24. George, *Presidential Decisionmaking*, 228.

25. Sundquist, *Decline and Resurgence*, 291.

26. Hamilton, "Congress and Foreign Policy," 136; Destler, "Executive-Congressional Conflict," 298; Brenner, *Limits and Possibilities*, 91.

27. Sundquist, *Decline and Resurgence*, 275.

28. Charles O. Jones, *An Introduction to the Study of Public Policy* (North Scituate, Mass.: Duxbury Press, 1977), 49.

29. Larry N. Gerston, *Making Public Policy: From Conflict to Resolution* (Glenview, Ill.: Scott, Foresman, 1983), 95.

30. Jones, *Study of Public Policy*, 139, and Robert L. Lineberry, *American Public Policy* (New York: Harper & Row, 1977), 70-71.

31. Jones, *Study of Public Policy*, 139.

32. "Joint Resolution to Keep Marines in Lebanon" (text of S. J. Res. 159), *Congressional Quarterly Weekly Report*, October 8, 1983, 2101.
33. "Address to Nation on Lebanon, Grenada," ibid., October 29, 1983, 2273-2275. See also John Felton, "Redeployment Fails to Quell Anger, Doubts," ibid., February 11, 1984, 239-241, and "Assigning the Blame for Outcome in Lebanon," ibid., February 18, 1984, 301-303.
34. I. M. Destler, "Trade Consensus, SALT Stalemate: Congress and Foreign Policy in the 1970s," in *The New Congress*, ed. Thomas E. Mann and Norman J. Ornstein (Washington, D.C.: American Enterprise Institute, 1981), 329.
35. Ibid., 356.
36. Thomas M. Franck and Edward Weisband, *Foreign Policy by Congress* (New York: Oxford University Press, 1979), 3.
37. Crabb and Holt, *Invitation to Struggle*, 243.
38. Ibid., 243-244.
39. John Spanier and Eric M. Uslaner, *How American Foreign Policy Is Made* (New York: Praeger, 1978), 3.
40. Crabb and Holt, *Invitation to Struggle*, 244.
41. Kenneth N. Waltz, *Foreign Policy and Democratic Politics* (Boston: Little, Brown, 1967), 13-14.
42. Ibid., 20.
43. Paula Stern, *Water's Edge: Domestic Politics and the Making of American Foreign Policy* (Westport, Conn.; Greenwood, 1979).
44. Unnamed representative, quoted in Godfrey Hodgson, *Congress and American Foreign Policy* (London: Royal Institute of International Affairs, 1979), 11, as cited in Sundquist, *Decline and Resurgence*, 285.
45. Jerrold E. Schneider, *Ideological Coalitions in Congress* (Westport, Conn.: Greenwood, 1979), 196 and chaps. 3 and 5.
46. Brenner, *Limits and Possibilities*, 94.
47. Waltz, *Foreign Policy*, 305.
48. Franck and Weisband, *Foreign Policy by Congress*, 85.
49. Crabb and Holt, *Invitation to Struggle*, 188.
50. Franck and Weisband, *Foreign Policy by Congress*, 211, and Sundquist, *Decline and Resurgence*, 298.
51. Crabb and Holt, *Invitation to Struggle*, 96.
52. Franck and Weisband, *Foreign Policy by Congress*, 8.

Economic Policy and the Congressional Budget Process | 8

Economic policy, like foreign policy, is an area of high visibility and national interest. The two differ, however, in the relative importance given to constituency interests. Although such interests may be factors in the making of foreign policy, they are considerably more important in economic policy making. When pressures are exerted by constituents in an adversarial system, serious problems for the economy can arise. Partly in an effort to deal with them, Congress has enacted a new budget process. From the adversary-unitary perspective, the results have been mixed, and Congress's ability to resist adversary pressures in economic policy making remains questionable.

Budgetary Effects of Adversary Pressures

It is not difficult to see how adversary pressures arise as Congress develops the annual federal budget. Individuals, groups, and districts are interested in receiving program benefits from government, and they also seek loopholes or preferences that will limit their taxes. Particular programs or tax preferences may be in the national interest, but if many of them are enacted the result is a budgetary deficit, as revenues fall short of expenditures. In times of economic recovery, this deficit can have a recessionary impact; government competes with the private sector for a limited supply of credit, driving up interest rates and slowing economic growth. On the other hand, if the Federal Reserve Board, a quasi-independent agency, increases the supply of credit in the economy to meet both government and private demand, the impact may be inflationary, as more money chases a limited supply of goods. Thus, a large government deficit can adversely affect the nation's economy and in that way the national interest. While the state of the economy is not the only criterion to use in determining the national interest, it is clearly an important one.

Certain adversary tendencies in Congress exacerbate the tendency toward large deficits. For example, the politics of inclusion, by which particular program benefits are distributed to most congressional districts regardless of need (see chapters 3 and 5), does build congressional majorities, but it also can lead to excessive spending. Similarly, the norm of reciprocity, by which support for programs and tax benefits is traded, increases expenditures and reduces revenues. Both of these patterns exist partly because congressional parties are not strong enough to produce majorities without them. Thus, the weakness of congressional parties indirectly contributes to deficits.

Other aspects of the adversary process in Congress also contribute to high expenditures.[1] Many programs provide benefits to small groups, for whom the advantages are great, and at the same time distribute the costs of these programs (taxes) over large numbers of people, so that the per capita cost of any program is small.[2] Program beneficiaries therefore support sympathetic legislators with votes and perhaps campaign contributions, while voters in general have little incentive to punish members and may not even know what they did. This disparity between the perceptions of the costs and benefits of particular programs has led some analysts to conclude that the nation's economy will tend to have an overly large public sector.[3] Whether or not one agrees with that judgment, it does alert us to an important factor in high public expenditures. Logrolling or vote-trading arrangements also facilitate such expenditures. These trades can occur because the costs of these agreements are often imposed on third parties, the millions of taxpayers, in general, while their benefits are concentrated on particular groups, at little direct cost to them. Members concerned about reelection and support therefore have strong incentives to represent constituents in a way that favors beneficiaries over those paying for programs. Because legislators respond to organized and informed interests and to visible beneficiaries, more than to the less visible and knowledgeable individuals who pay for the programs, they participate in a distortion of the adversary process whereby some individual and district interests are represented more effectively than others. The outcome of all of these forces is high public expenditures.

Options in Financing Government Programs

Congress can strive for a balance between expenditures and revenues in any of four ways: (1) by reducing or eliminating existing programs; (2) by raising taxes; (3) by borrowing funds; and (4) by using additional revenue generated by economic growth.[4] The choice among these methods is affected by legislators' preferences for distributing benefits as visibly as possible and costs as invisibly as possible. The first option will therefore often be rejected, since eliminating or curtailing a program creates a visible class of losers, who are not likely to suffer quietly. The second option also punishes a visible class, the targeted taxpayers, who are sometimes a well-informed and well-organized group. For example, gasoline and social security taxes are relatively transparent and may produce strong negative reaction. On the other hand, Congress is sometimes able to disguise tax increases and thereby fund larger expenditures with little opposition. This has been especially true during inflationary periods, when tax revenues rise even without any change in tax rates. This occurs because taxpayers are pushed into higher tax brackets even if their real (inflation-adjusted) incomes have not changed.[5] Since few individual programs are large enough to represent a sizable portion of the federal budget, tax hikes for any one program need not be especially large or visible. This makes tax increases a preferred, though not the most preferred way to finance increases in program benefits.

The third option, borrowing money, or "deficit financing," works even better to disguise program costs. If the Federal Reserve System refuses to allow growth in the money supply to accommodate the borrowing, the government deficit will force interest rates to rise. If the Federal Reserve System does allow growth in the money supply, the result may be greater inflation. In either case, the costs of a spending program are obscured, for the impact is primarily macroeconomic, working through the entire economy. Workers and consumers are rarely able to attribute the costs of slow growth and inflation to specific government spending programs. It may even be difficult for them to attribute their economic plight to congressional action at all. Which unemployed workers can say their job loss resulted from weak capital formation as a consequence of federal borrowing rather than from other economic forces? Which consumers can say how much of the erosion in their real income can be attributed to excessive borrowing by the federal treasury rather than to changes in labor markets?

Deficit financing not only disguises the costs of public programs; it also divorces those who pay for them from their beneficiaries. Since winners and losers are separate, and losers are invisible while winners are prominent, the system moves toward large deficits. Congressional deliberation will frequently pit the political force of an interest group intensely dedicated to securing tangible benefits against the muted resistance of a large class of people who will pay for those benefits, but none of whom perceives significant harm from a particular piece of legislation.

The fourth option, financing programs out of the revenues generated by economic growth, can obviously help both to avoid deficit financing and to disguise costs. Such growth, however, has not always occurred with sufficient vigor to fund all the desired programs, and so Congress is forced to choose among the first three options.

The Congressional Budget Process

Members of Congress have been aware of the problems created by the pressures described above and have tried to face them. One effort in that direction was the Budget and Impoundment Act of 1974, which can be regarded as a unitary move to deal with the effects of the adversary system. As noted earlier (see chapter 4), this act was developed at a time when the appropriations and tax-policy committees were becoming less effective as agents of control in Congress. The weakening of committee function reflected increased pressure within and on Congress for higher spending and tax-benefit increases, and the budget act can be seen as an attempt to create new controls to replace the old. A slowing economy at the time reinforced the need for budgetary controls.

The budget act established new House and Senate budget committees.[6] These committees were given responsibility for producing two budget resolutions a year, one to be adopted before consideration of spending and revenue legislation for the coming fiscal year, the other to be passed shortly before the start of the fiscal year. The first resolution was to provide spending and revenue targets but did not prevent Congress from making any spending or revenue decisions it wanted. The second was to set a ceiling on total budget outlays and a floor on total revenues. Once the second resolution had been passed, Congress was not supposed to violate these self-imposed budget constraints. It could, however, pass a third budget resolution at any time during the fiscal year to revise previous decisions.[7]

Expenditures and revenues were to be treated differently in the budget resolutions. Total spending (outlays and budgetary authority) was divided into 19 categories, such as agriculture, health, and defense. In contrast, only total revenue and the amount by which it was to be increased or decreased by changes in the tax code had to be included in the resolutions. Under the new process, the budget committees were expected to keep close watch on the legislation being developed by the other committees, to provide information on its budgetary impact and on the status of the budget generally, and to keep the two houses and their legislative and appropriations committees informed on whether particular measures conformed with the latest budget resolution.

This new budget process has forced Congress to consider total revenues and expenditures and the consequent deficit (or surplus) they produce. Total expenditures in the budget resolutions are required to include "backdoor" or uncontrollable spending. Backdoor spending refers to funds disbursed by agencies and programs without going through the normal channels of congressional appropriations. Entitlement programs make up the largest part of this spending. Social security is one example: Since both the right to receive benefits and the level of benefits received are specified by law, Congress cannot control social security expenditure without changing the law itself. Uncontrollable spending currently accounts for more than half of every dollar the national government lays out in domestic spending.[8]

The budget act required Congress to estimate total expenditures, including uncontrollable spending; then to estimate revenues under existing law; and finally to consider the projected deficit. Thus, Congress has the obligation and the opportunity to consider alternative levels of expenditures, revenues, and deficits and to develop a broad economic approach. Before the 1974 act, Congress would authorize, appropriate, and tax in many separate actions, with little attention given to the totals involved or their fiscal effects, and with one part of Congress not paying much attention to actions by other parts.

Under the new process, the Budget committees have been required to provide five-year estimates of the costs of current actions, which allows Congress to get a sense of the future impact of its decisions. The requirement that spending be specified within 19 categories has also given Congress the opportunity to face explicitly the question of priorities. On the other hand, the 19 spending categories were not the same as those used by the Appropriations committees, which gave those committees some leeway in what they did. Similar leeway was given to the tax committees by the requirement that only total revenue be listed in budget resolutions. The new process was a self-imposed congressional discipline and an opportunity for change. The question, of course, was whether that process would achieve the broad, unitary goals implicit in the act.

During the first five years of the act (1975-1979), Congress passed what have been called "accommodating" budgets.[9] Congress did not shift monies between its 19 categories except in a very marginal way during this period. Explicit tradeoffs between functions were avoided; each was treated as a discrete policy choice. Rather than cut funds for particular functions, Congress set different rates of growth for various parts of the budget, the same practice followed before 1974. Those who had hoped that the new process would hold down expenditures were disappointed. Most of the savings that were supposed to result from the first budget resolutions were not achieved.[10] On the other hand, no new entitlement programs were passed during these years. Program initiatives were discouraged, as Congress was reluctant to raise the deficit much beyond the president's estimate and unwilling to sharply cut existing programs in order to be able to fund new ones.

These "accommodating" budgets can be explained by Congress's continued use of adversary democratic processes. According to one close observer of the process, "Most Members have strong feelings about only a few of the items in [the budget]. If they are satisfied about these and not deeply disturbed by the total spending and deficit levels, they can be persuaded to vote for the budget resolutions."[11] By voting down amendments calling for explicit transfers between categories, as they repeatedly did, members sought to mitigate conflict. The practice of distributive politics allowed satisfaction of a wide variety of interests and in that way produced budget resolutions that could pass. By taking up categories one at a time, without first setting overall spending targets, the Budget committees tried to protect individual and district interests in the same way as in past congressional action. Adjusting budgets in a marginal way had the same effect. Of course, this process did not necessarily assure equal protection of interests; interests previously left out in the distribution of benefits did not gain much from these changes at the margins.

From a unitary perspective, the first years of the budget process left something to be desired. A restructuring of national priorities was not seriously considered. While the process focused more attention than previously on the deficit, the savings that were expected in first budget resolutions were, by and large, not achieved. Instead of seriously considering broad alternative budgets, Congress tinkered with marginal changes. While the political reasons for this are apparent and reflect the adversary forces within Congress, unitary considerations that might have surfaced in the new process seem to have been given short shrift. The potential for discipline in the first resolutions was not realized by the authorizing, appropriating, and tax committees; instead, Congress simply modified initial targets with adjustments in the second and third budget resolutions. Even after second budget resolutions were passed, Congress did not abide by the spending ceilings and revenue floors that were set.

The Use of Reconciliation

The budget act also included a "reconciliation" procedure, a method of enforcing the spending ceilings and revenue floor of the second budget resolution. If, as a result of the economy and Congress's own actions, total spending and revenue deviated from what the second resolution posited, Congress could instruct its committees to propose changes to eliminate the discrepancies. A reconciliation instruction, passed by the full chamber, could tell committees to make changes that would achieve specified reductions in spending or specified increases in revenues. The committees would then report their proposals to the Budget Committee, which would combine them into a single reconciliation bill and send it to the floor, where it was subject to amendment prior to final passage.

Thus, the second budget resolution allowed Congress to modify the total spending that would be brought about by its decisions, previous laws, and the state of the economy, and then to enforce that modification through reconciliation. Congress did not use reconciliation in this way before 1980. While specific expenditure reductions were assumed in the first resolutions and included in Budget Committee reports as assumptions underlying projected savings, they were not part of the actual resolutions Congress voted on. Consequently, the legislative committees usually failed to propose changes in the law that would achieve the savings.

As a result, Budget Committee members began to consider using reconciliation in connection with the first budget resolution. To further the discipline Congress imposed on itself, a number of members were willing to support such a change. In 1980, the Carter administration and a congressional delegation agreed to use reconciliation in this way. The reconciliation measure instructed various committees to make program cuts totaling about $8 billion, and the committees generally conformed their proposals to these instructions.

A much more substantial use of reconciliation tied to the first resolution was made in 1981, after the Reagan administration had taken office. In initial reconciliation instructions, the House and Senate directed 30 committees to make reductions of about $145 billion for the fiscal years 1982 through 1984. Each committee was given an amount it was to cut over each of the three years, and suggestions were made as to what program reductions or changes might accomplish these savings. The committees were given 22 days to report back legislation. They had discretion as to which programs to change or eliminate to achieve the cuts, but the size of the required savings limited that discretion. Under the budget act, the Budget committees could not modify these recommendations. They combined them into a single bill, which in this instance was replaced on the floor by a substitute bill. The substitute made reductions in 250 of approximately 1,000 federal programs. It was the longest bill in congressional history and contained the largest cuts ever made in domestic spending.

The significance of this use of reconciliation is that it circumvented the normal legislative process. In the absence of reconciliation, the cuts proposed by the Reagan administration would have been considered by the pertinent authorizing and appropriating committees, after the usual hearings. Legislative action would have taken place in 30 or more committees, producing a large number of bills for floor consideration. Some committees would have done little or nothing about suggested cuts. Because of the political climate, some of the cuts the president had requested would have been accepted, but the sheer number of suggested reductions made it unlikely that he would have gotten them all. Members would have had leeway to vote with the president on some matters and against him on others. Interest groups and committees loyal to particular programs could have mustered their forces in many arenas of action. With reconciliation, on the other hand, the president had to win only twice: on the initial instruction and on the omnibus reconciliation bill. With that one bill, President Reagan and his supporting majority in Congress were able to modify 250 programs.

The reconciliation process had obvious adversary significance. By consolidating many program changes into one bill, it limited members' opportunities to vote for the interests of their constituencies. Instead of dealing with relatively small packages of legislation, which could be amended separately, legislators were confronted with a massive bill, with only a limited number of amendments allowed. They therefore had fewer opportunities to vote on particular parts of the overall bill and were faced with far more aggregated choices. Because the initial reconciliation instructions sharply constrained authorizing committees by establishing required spending cuts, the leverage of those committees and their clientele was weakened. Because the final reconciliation bill similarly limited appropriations committees to these lower authorization levels, those committees were less able to function as courts of appeal. As a result, individual, group, and district interests, and their congressional defenders, were checked in what they could achieve in committee and on the floor.[12]

Adversary democracy can take a variety of forms. Members can attempt to represent individuals equally while utilizing the principle of majority rule in the legislature. The problem with this is that minorities can get outvoted and not receive benefits proportional to their numbers. Adversary democracy can also strive for equal representation of interests through a process of "taking turns," which allows diverse interests to be accommodated at least to some degree if not with complete equality (see chapters 4 and 5). Omnibus reconciliation bills tied to first budget resolutions threaten this process of taking turns; politically weaker interests, previously represented, can lose in the larger arena of conflict—as happened, for example, to the working poor in 1981. By the same token, the influence of numerous special interests can be reduced.[13] Thus, even programs favoring such fairly strong groups as farmers, veterans, and small business have been threatened by the budget process.

Another effect of reconciliation is that it substantially increases parent-chamber control over committees. Legislative committees can be instructed to provide three-year program authorizations at levels below the funding those programs had previously received from appropriations committees, and thus be sharply limited as advocates of discretionary spending. Similarly, reconciliation instructions can greatly reduce the options of appropriations committees. To the extent that the chambers are more representative of the nation as a whole than their committees are (committees vary in this regard—see chapter 4), the reconciliation decisions of the chambers would be more representative. Of course, various minorities may well not receive benefits proportional to their numbers or to the intensity of their interests; reconciliation tied to the first budget resolution reduces the impact of factors such as intensity of preferences and effectiveness of organization.

Use of reconciliation with the first budget resolution also has important unitary implications. Members and observers have suggested that the reconciliation process does not permit legislation to be understood and considered to the same degree as does the normal legislative process. Too many matters are included in a single bill, and too little time is given to committees to achieve instructed budget cuts. Because amendments are strictly limited, especially in the House, members are not in a position to evaluate carefully and act on many parts of the overall bill. This constrains unitary as well as adversary democracy. Reconciliation limits opportunities members have to vote their views; they are required to vote yes or no on a whole package, with only limited amendments. On the other hand, critics who point out that sufficient consideration of legislation is not encouraged under reconciliation often fail to note that committees, which would otherwise be the major focus of careful attention, often are influenced by special interests.

Reconciliation and the entire budget process may also have a negative effect on unitary democracy by contributing to what has been called the "fiscalization" of congressional debate.[14] In place of a search for a balance between program and financial values, financial concerns tend to predominate. Debate is sometimes focused less on the merits of a program than on whether it is or will remain within a budget target. This emphasis on fiscal matters no doubt reflects the current political climate and members' concern about the economy, but the budget process certainly reinforces that trend.

But reconciliation also has positive unitary aspects. Because members vote on omnibus bills including many items, they can more easily vote for what they consider to be good public policy, even if it is unpopular. They can explain their vote by saying they did not like every part of the reconciliation bill, especially the elimination of or reductions in a program favored by some constituents, but a positive vote on the whole package of budget cuts was needed to reduce the deficit.

Reconciliation attached to the first budget resolution, as in 1981, can limit government spending. The $145 billion cut in domestic spending, combined with the $43 billion increase in military spending approved at the same time, produced a net saving of $102 billion over three years. For those who believe that reduced government spending is necessary, the reconciliation process may well be seen as facilitating the national interest. Those who believe that Congress should be active in ordering national priorities might also react positively to the changes of 1981. A real increase in defense expenditures of 10 percent, as well as the massive domestic cuts, demonstrated that Congress is not necessarily confined to tinkering at the margins. Some have argued that this capacity to shift priorities has made Congress more responsive to changing public opinion.[15] It seems clear that it also contributes to the unitary dimension of congressional democracy.

Nevertheless, because reconciliation so threatens the influence of the authorizing and appropriating committees, of subcommittees, and of individual members and interests, it is hard to conceive of members tolerating regular use of the process. The influence of individual members and their leeway in dealing with constituents and various interests are too sharply constrained by reconciliation for members to accept it as the norm. Reconciliation also enhances the president's power, because he has to win fewer votes, and that sits uneasily with some members. Extraordinary situations, in which great premium is placed on substantial reductions in government spending, might again lead to the employment of reconciliation as an instrument for achieving them. But in normal times, adversary pressures from interests and members are likely to be too great to permit this.

Net Effects of the Budget Process

One of the ironies of the 1981 experience with reconciliation is that it can be viewed as contributing to an increase in government budget deficits, even though the new congressional budget process had been widely regarded as a useful tool for reducing those deficits. The huge tax cut proposed by the Reagan administration and approved in 1981—a reduction of $750 billion over a five-year period—probably would not have passed Congress if substantial cuts in spending had not also been made. But because total revenue reductions greatly exceeded spending reductions, the deficits projected for the 1980s rose considerably. During 1984, for example, the federal government lost about $120 billion in revenues as a result of the 1981 tax cut, and that was a major reason for the 1984 deficit of $190 billion. While those who believe in supply-side economics and those favoring reduced government spending supported the 1981 policy, it remains true that the budget process effectively added to, rather than reduced, the federal deficit. This is not to say, however, that the process might not have an opposite effect. By consolidating spending cuts and tax increases, the budget process could be used to produce policies whose overall effect is deficit reduction.

Although the budget process is important in shaping the fiscal policies of government spending, taxation, and deficit management, there is a question as to how important those policies are to the general state of the economy—and it is because of their effects on the economy that legislators are concerned about them. Economists disagree about the precise roles and relative importance of fiscal and monetary policy in the economy. (Monetary policy, as distinct from fiscal policy, refers to the decisions, especially those taken by the Federal Reserve Board, that affect the supply of money and credit.) There is general agreement that a weakness in Congress's use of spending and taxation to strengthen the economy is their delayed effect. By the time spending and program cuts pass and are implemented, a year or more may have gone by since Congress diagnosed the economic situation and decided what to do about it. Monetary policy, on the other hand, has much more immediate, and some say stronger, effects.[16] There is also the question of whether Congress is willing to support unpopular economic policies. Congress (as well as some presidents) has been reluctant to enact the spending cuts and tax increases that might be necessary to reduce inflation.

The Federal Reserve Board, however, can do what Congress is reluctant to do—for example, reduce the supply of money. In doing so, the Federal Reserve can serve unitary goals that might otherwise be hard to achieve. While Congress and presidents have sometimes been critical of Federal Reserve policies, they generally have not attempted to reduce the board's independence. As an institution with unitary characteristics, the Federal Reserve system can compensate for the difficulty Congress has in taking certain actions. By generally supporting the Federal Reserve and not seeking to control monetary policy, Congress serves unitary ends by delegation.

Summary

Examination of economic policy and the congressional budget process reveals a pattern that has been seen before, one of tension between adversary and unitary tendencies in Congress. The new budget process represents one of the stronger unitary mechanisms in Congress. That process has been used, especially when reconciliation was tied to the first budget resolution, to produce congressional action on the economy that was markedly different from previous actions and that has interesting implications for unitary and adversary democracy. The budget process is a unitary mechanism Congress can use to control its adversary excesses. But precisely because forceful use of reconciliation limits adversary pressures and the capacity of members to protect interests, Congress is not likely to accept reconciliation as the norm. It is in this way that Congress works through an adversary-unitary dialectic in its economic policy making.

NOTES

1. The authors wish to thank Professor Michael Weinstein of the Economics Department of Haverford College for his help with this part of the analysis. See also Brian Barry, *Political Argument* (London: Routledge & Kegan Paul, 1965), 318, and Edgar K. Browning and Jacqueline M. Browning, *Public Finance and the Price System* (New York: Macmillan, 1979).

2. Programs of this kind are frequently referred to as "distributive"; see Randall B. Ripley and Grace A. Franklin, *Congress, the Bureaucracy, and Public Policy* (Homewood, Ill.: Dorsey, 1980), 16-18, and Theodore Lowi, "American Business, Public Policy, Case Studies, and Political Theory," *World Politics* 16 (July 1964): 689-690.

3. Peter Aranson, "Deficits in Normative Economics and Positive Political Theory," in *The Economic Consequences of Government Deficits*, ed. Laurence Meyer (Boston: Kluwer-Nijhoff, 1983), 157-182, and Roger Noll, "Discussion," in ibid., 201-210.

4. Again, we thank Professor Weinstein for his help in the analysis of the choices Congress faces in financing programs.

5. The tax-indexing plan that is scheduled to go into effect in 1985 is meant to end this. The Reagan administration, which sought to limit spending by limiting tax revenues, proposed this plan in 1981, and it was accepted by Congress.

6. This account follows Allen Schick, "The Three-Ring Budget Process: The Appropriations, Tax, and Budget Committees in Congress," in *The New Congress*, ed. Thomas E. Mann and Norman J. Ornstein (Washington, D.C.: American Enterprise Institute, 1981), 311-313.

7. From 1982 through 1984, Congress passed no second budget resolution. Rather, members set targets in the first resolution, which they did not always follow. In 1984, Congress did not agree on the first resolution until late in the year, after several appropriations bills and a major tax increase had been passed. These are examples of how congressional practice has deviated from what was prescribed in the act. The text describes the way in which the process is supposed to work under the act, in order to highlight its unitary aspects. Later in the chapter, there is a discussion of the ways in which adversary pressures limited what it could achieve.

8. David J. Vogler, *The Politics of Congress*, 4th ed. (Boston: Allyn & Bacon, 1983), 184.

9. The term and the analysis underlying it are from Allen Schick, *Congress and Money* (Washington, D.C.: Urban Institute, 1980), 331-356. For other assessments of the workings of the act during this period, see John W. Ellwood, "Budget Control in a Redistributive Environment," in *Making Economic Policy in Congress*, ed. Allen Schick (Washington, D.C.: American Enterprise Institute, 1983), 69-99; Louis Fisher, "Congressional Budget Reform: The First Two Years," *Harvard Journal on Legislation* 14 (April 1977): 413-457; Joel Havemann, *Congress and the Budget* (Bloomington: Indiana University Press, 1978); and James A. Thurber, "New Powers of the Purse: An Assessment of Congressional Budget Reform," in *Legislative Reform: The Policy Impact*, ed. Leroy N. Rieselbach (Lexington, Mass.: Lexington Books, 1978), 159-172.

10. Allen Schick, *Reconciliation and the Congressional Budget Process* (Washington, D.C.: American Enterprise Institute, 1981), 5-7.
11. Schick, *Congress and Money*, 338.
12. For more detail on how reconciliation limits the authorizing and appropriations processes, see Schick, *Reconciliation*, 41-42. As he points out, the reconciliation bill changed laws so that authorized spending was significantly less than previous appropriations. For many programs it covered a three-year period, and in numerous cases the changes were permanent. The authorizing committees had their alternatives limited both by the initial reconciliation instruction and by the final bill. The appropriations committees, which cannot appropriate more money than has been authorized, also had their options sharply restrained.
13. Thus, reconciliation achieves part of what some had hoped political parties would produce.
14. Schick, *Reconciliation*, 35.
15. Ibid., 31.
16. One place where the limited economic utility of Congress's fiscal policies can be seen is in its handling of recessions. The government responds "automatically" to recessions through programs already in place, such as unemployment insurance and welfare, whose payouts increase during an economic downturn. Congress can also take additional counterrecessionary measures, such as increasing unemployment insurance and welfare, lowering taxes, and increasing spending on public works, revenue sharing for states, job training, and public employment programs. According to some economists who have studied these discretionary programs, their net fiscal impact is small. The stimulus they provide does not seem to affect the overall timing or magnitude of recovery in the business cycle. For an example of this view, see Wilfred Lewis, *Federal Fiscal Policy in the Postwar Recessions* (Washington, D.C.: Brookings Institution, 1962).

Conclusions 9

Three questions have guided the discussion and analysis through-out this book: How does the framework of adversary and unitary democracy help us to understand the national legislature? How does it help us to evaluate both the institution and its members? How does it help us to judge the relationship between congressional behavior and democratic legitimacy? The preceding chapters have described patterns of legislative behavior and suggested points of analysis relevant to the answers. This chapter reviews the major conclusions of the book in light of those three questions.

Understanding Congress

In chapter 1, the adversary-unitary perspective was used to analyze congressional action on immigration reform. Reviews of the defeat of the Simpson-Mazzoli bill in conference after both chambers had passed different versions of it tended to stress adversary aspects of the congressional process in explaining that defeat. The legislation failed, according to this interpretation, because "it had tried to accommodate too many interests and had gone too far in too many directions." [1] Or, in the words of a supporter of the bill, it was defeated because "the special interest prevails over the general interest." [2] Analysis of this case from a perspective of adversary democracy could take two distinct forms. One is that the bill failed because it did not meet the standards of adversary democracy, such as equal protection of interests. The other is that the bill became such an extreme form of accommodation of adversarial special interests that it failed to hold together as coherent policy. The first explanation indicates the value of the adversary framework; the second suggests its limits and leads to the recognition that something more than an adversary perspective is needed to understand and explain congressional behavior in this case.

The perspective of unitary democracy provides an alternative basis for explaining the bill's defeat in conference: its failure as coherent public policy. But the value of the unitary perspective becomes more apparent when the focus is shifted from the bill's defeat in conference to its committee and floor approval in both House and Senate. As one observer of those actions noted, the bill "wasn't passed by magic." [3] To ignore Congress's deliberative search for common interests and consensus would indeed leave important aspects of its behavior in the realm of "magic."

Perhaps the chief value of the two-democracies framework in the understanding of congressional behavior is to be found more in the questions it raises than in the answers it provides. What effects do different notions of a public or national interest have on the behavior of legislators? By what standards can the representativeness of the institution be measured? How valid are the claims that the presidency is the sole or primary political institution that perceives and acts in the national interest? What types of committees and committee activity serve to develop awareness of common interests? What types of concerns govern members' actions on the floor? What information is transmitted in the cue system and why is face-to-face interaction among members important to that system? How effective is Congress in developing economic and foreign policies that are shaped by visions of the national interest?

Throughout the book, instances have been seen where conceptions of a common or national interest appear to be motivating the actions of political leaders and where a national interest is asserted as being something more than the sum of individual or district interests. Aspects of congressional deliberation have been observed that suggest a legislative process that is different from the popular image of bargaining and logrolling by representatives of conflicting interests. An awareness of the unitary as well as the adversary side of Congress is essential to an understanding of that institution, and it provides richer and more realistic grounds for evaluating congressional performance and for perceiving the relationship between congressional behavior and democratic legitimacy.

Evaluating Congress

In 1977, the House Commission on Administrative Review reported on two surveys conducted under its direction: a national survey of public opinion on Congress by pollster Lou Harris and a survey of a representative sample of 153 House members in the 95th Congress (1977-1978). The parallel nature of the surveys permitted comparison of public and member opinions. When asked to name the most important duties or functions of the congressional job, 45 percent of the members put "looking after the needs and interests of the nation as a whole" in first place, and 24 percent gave first priority to constituency service and district representation; among the general public, 57 percent said that the top priority of members of Congress should be looking after their district and only 34 percent gave that position to national interests.[4]

The importance of Congress as a deliberative body with a responsibility to produce legislation in the national interest is a concept that its members regularly employ in evaluating the institution. Sen. John C. Stennis, D-Miss., commenting on the changes he had seen in his 36 years as a senator, said:

> Something very elusive has gotten away from us. We do not listen to each other as much as we should. We do not have a proper chance to talk to each other. That has been lost; I do not know exactly where, but lost. It is not here anymore. In fact, [the Senate] has lost much in the way of ability to debate and be heard, transmit ideas to other leaders and thereby produce conclusions.[5]

Sen. Howard H. Baker, Jr., R-Tenn., offered a similar assessment: "I think it is a matter of national loss that the Senate as a body has forfeited a great amount of its status as the nation's prime forum for the debate of public issues."[6] The concern for legislation directed toward a national interest is evident in remarks by two House members. Too often, said one, "we act in response to interest groups. In seeking their vote and support, we are acting in our own self-interest, rather than that of the nation."[7] And House majority leader Wright has warned of the danger "in the tendency of increasing numbers of people to think of themselves and their special interests first, and only second in terms of the national interests of the country."[8]

Yet in order to remain in office, senators and representatives must be successful in responding to voters' ideas about what members of

Congress should be doing, and so it is clearly in their electoral interest to yield to the district-first values held by the public. Fenno found that important aspects of members' "home style" were both a stress on constituency representation and a disassociation of themselves from the negative public opinion about Congress. Members tend to campaign for Congress either by running "against" the institution or by simply ignoring it and concentrating instead on their value as representatives for the district. This is true even when members speak to people whose support they already have. "Representatives do very little," Fenno discovered, "to help their supportive constituents to conceptualize the House as an institution." [9] The analysis presented throughout this book, on the other hand, shows that evaluation of congressional democracy in unitary terms requires just that sort of conceptualization.

As long as the standards used by the public for evaluating congressional performance are primarily adversarial and are applied to individual representatives, there is not much incentive for change. Members will continue to have grounds for criticizing the institutional shortcomings of Congress. But adversary standards need not be the only ones used by the public to judge congressional democracy. The rhetoric of presidential campaigns and of the presidency regularly displays the ideas of unitary democracy and shows that the public can respond in those terms. The discussion in chapter 3 of the expectations made of presidents and presidential candidates on the issue of immigration reform is one such illustration of those unitary standards. The response to President Reagan's proposed 1986 budget by Senator Dole (a fellow Republican and Senate majority leader) suggests that there are times when members of Congress aspire to standards more clearly unitary than those governing presidential behavior. President Reagan's budget message to Congress, according to Senator Dole, essentially said: "Don't touch Social Security. Don't touch defense. Don't raise taxes. And you can't touch interest on the [national] debt. That doesn't leave a great deal. Those of us in the Congress have to maybe look beyond some of the President's promises of the campaign." [10]

Members of Congress who seek congressional change in the direction of unitary democracy would benefit from attempts to educate constituents, to help them conceptualize the institution and understand the relevance to it of the values of unitary democracy. Members might, for example, help constituents realize the importance of consensus to congressional policy making. Legislators and those who write about the institution regularly employ that concept in describing it. Representative Hamilton, for example, has said, "The toughest thing to do in this institution is to build consensus." An explanation for the 1984 stalemate on immigration reform put forward by Representative Hyde echoed that view: "The legislative process worked. But there was an ambivalence that could not produce the necessary consensus for any version of the bill." [11] As Congress ended its 1983 session, a reporter referred to "the widespread belief in Congress that there exists no political consensus that could lead the way to further domestic spending cuts of the magnitude needed to close the deficit." A year later, congressional stalemate on a number of issues was explained in this way: "Congress operates by public consensus, and this year such consensus proved elusive on issues ranging from military spending to immigration to civil rights." [12] A student of congressional policy making has written, "More effectively than any other institution of government, [Congress] works to nurture consensus—indeed, in a broad sense, that is its most important contribution to the polity." [13] Another has suggested that "Congress's actions or inactions represent the consensus—or lack thereof—in the country at large. . . . Where and when there has been a national consensus, Congress has acted, reasonably quickly and reasonably well." [14]

A distinction that emerges from these observations is that between an institutional consensus and a consensus among the general public. The two are obviously linked, but it is important to recognize that congressional consensus can be a product of legislative deliberation as well as of constituent representation. Existence of a policy consensus within Congress need not, of course, be taken to mean that there is a similar consensus among constituents. [15] But the building of such a public consensus is a task that legislators might undertake. They can do this by representing the institution to their constituents, just as they regularly do the opposite. By telling constituents about both the adversary claims of other representatives and constitutents and the institutional process of consensus building, members can have an impact on both the substance and the public understanding of congressional policies.

In chapters 2 and 3, there was a discussion of the control that members have over explanations of individual and congressional behavior offered to their constituents and how those explanations can fit both adversary and unitary models of democracy. For example, adversary accounts of congressional action can be used to explain why the member was unable to get any or all of what constituents wanted in a particular policy area. Describing the diversity of interests involved in an issue can provide a rationale for the outcome and enhance constituents' evaluation of members' actions. Constituents have some interest in adversary explanations, since that is how most of them view congressional politics. They may also be responsive to explanations that focus on the equal protection of interests, the primary standard of adversary democracy, since that standard fits both with their conception of democracy and their idea of fairness. Acceptance of the adversary standard of equal protection is what Rep. Silvio O. Conte, R-Mass., was implying when he reported the reaction in his district to proposed cuts in the budget: "My constituents tell me they're willing to take their lumps if everybody else takes theirs." [16]

By building on constituents' predisposition to think of politics in adversary terms and leading them to apply adversary standards to the institution as a whole rather than only to individual legislators, members could greatly improve the quality and value of public assessments of Congress. Educating constituents in this way would also help to move Congress and the process of representation closer to Madison's conception of the House of Representatives "as a substitute for a meeting of the citizens in person." [17] Such an effort, by involving constituents as well as members in a search for common interests and consensus, would also broaden the scope of unitary deliberation. Members have the opportunity to make public evaluation of the institution of Congress more realistic and valuable by pointing out this link between adversary and unitary standards of evaluation. It permits members to heed the warning of Jane Mansbridge that one cannot "throw away the half of human experience that values unitary goods and judge a polity solely on adversary criteria." [18]

Democratic Legitimacy

Legitimacy is a term with both descriptive and normative meanings. It is used both to describe public attitudes about the right of political leaders to make decisions and to justify their authority in terms of particular values. Although this book has touched on some aspects of descriptive legitimacy in considering public attitudes toward Congress, its major focus has been on the normative sense of the concept. Since congressional authority is justified by reference to democratic values, a discussion of different models of democracy and democratic values is bound to raise questions about the legitimacy of Congress.

The descriptive and normative meanings of legitimacy are obviously intertwined, and social commentators often use the term in both senses when discussing the legitimacy of particular institutions or regimes, or when referring to a general "legitimacy crisis." [19] The political legitimacy of the U.S. Supreme Court, for example, is said to rest on a pattern of judicial review that generates public acceptance over the long run and can be reconciled with the democratic principle of majority rule.[20] The legitimacy of the American presidency has been linked with economic growth, public support of such growth, and a particular conception of democracy that justifies executive power on grounds of sustained growth.[21]

The legitimacy of Congress, to a greater degree than these other institutions, rests on the values of representative democracy. But the values associated with adversary and unitary democracy, as has been seen throughout this book, are sufficiently different to create two separate bases of democratic legitimacy. In an adversarial sense, the democratic legitimacy of Congress is measured primarily by the accurate representation of district interests and a relative equality of power in protecting those interests. That is the meaning King seems to have had in mind when he pointed out that dependence on staff expertise and a stress on technical problem-solving can isolate legislators from constituents to the extent that their actions "lose the patina of democratic legitimacy." [22] Reforms of the 1970s that produced a more equitable distribution of power within Congress are "democratizing" reforms in the adversarial sense of equal protection of interests. The presence of another model for measuring democratic legitimacy, however, is suggested in this comment on the effects of those reforms offered by a member who supported them, Rep. Richard L. Ottinger, D-N.Y.: "The process that we tried to make very democratic is becoming very undemocratic." [23] By decentralizing and equalizing power within Congress, Ottinger was suggesting, the reforms had made creation of a congressional policy consensus more difficult.

The democratic legitimacy of Congress, in its unitary sense, depends not only on representation through elections but also on reaching policy agreement to deal with national problems. This notion of democratic legitimacy is implicit in discussions that raise questions about the "prestige" of Congress, its "effectiveness" as an institution, and the requirements of institutional maintenance. When Senator Mathias spoke of the institutional need to overcome delaying tactics in the 1982 postelection session of Congress, he was drawing on this set of values: "I think that most members of the Senate, and a high percentage of the general public, perceived that the Senate was unable to cope during the lame-duck session. If we were to continue as an effective institution, something had to be done." [24] Another example of this view of democratic legitimacy is David Mayhew's analysis of the behavior patterns needed to prevent the "decay or collapse" of Congress and to maintain the "prestige and power" of the institution.[25]

The policy decisions required to preserve the legitimacy of Congress are the products of both adversary and unitary processes. A policy decision, whether it is an adversary bargain struck among conflicting interests or a unitary agreement based on common interests, represents an end point of both types of democracy. The values of unitary democracy, however, seem more central to legitimacy in this sense than those of adversary democracy. Indeed, the patterns of behavior described by Mathias and by Mayhew can be said to maintain the effectiveness and legitimacy of Congress by checking the excesses of adversary democracy. But there is more to unitary democracy than that.

The democratic legitimacy of Congress rests on both the legislative process and the resulting policies. The value of unitary democracy is found not simply in widespread agreement or consensus but in the creative nature of the process itself. Members of Congress are expected to do more than represent the existing preferences of constituents and to work out bargains based on those preferences. This view of the legislative process as a creative one was reflected in a complaint made by former representative Eckhardt about the effect of reforms in congressional procedures. The House floor, he said, was "becoming more like the New York Stock Exchange than an area in which serious debate is possible—a place where transactions are made, but opinions are not changed by discussion." [26] The value of deliberation implicit in this remark lies in its dynamic nature, in the ability of the process to produce change and create new perceptions and even new interests. It is a view of the political process in which consensus is *created* rather than simply revealed. The perspective of unitary democracy, it has been suggested, leads to a conception of the political process "not as a struggle among interest groups equipped with preexisting preferences, but instead as an effort to develop and select those preferences in the form of shared public values. In other words, preferences are not necessarily filtered into the democratic process as exogenous variables; they are developed and shaped, indeed defined, during the political process." [27]

This conception of politics as a positive, creative process can be traced to Aristotle's views of citizenship and democracy and to some of Madison's writings on the Constitution.[28] As long as a substantial proportion of people view politics this way and value democracy in its unitary form, a congressional process that appears solely adversarial will lack legitimacy.

NOTES

1. Robert Pear, "Amid Charges, Immigration Bill Dies," *New York Times*, October 12, 1984, A16.
2. Rep. Charles E. Schumer, D-N.Y., quoted in ibid.
3. Maria Ochoa, a California delegate to the 1984 Democratic convention, quoted in Rob Gurwitt and Nadine Cohodas, "Hispanic-Asian Boycott: A Gesture Fizzles," *Congressional Quarterly Weekly Report*, July 21, 1984, 1733.
4. House Commission on Administrative Review, *Financial Ethics: Hearings and Meetings*, January 13, 14, and 31 and February 2 and 7, 1977, 192.
5. Quoted in Martin Tolchin, "Senators Assail Anarchy in New Chamber of Equals," *New York Times*, November 25, 1984, 40.
6. Quoted in ibid.
7. Unnamed representative quoted in "Exclusive Survey: What Congress Really Thinks of Itself," *U.S. News & World Report*, January 14, 1980, 39.
8. Quoted in Steven V. Roberts, "Hispanic Caucus Is Flexing Its Muscle," *New York Times*, October 10, 1983, 14.
9. Richard F. Fenno, Jr., *Home Style: House Members in Their Districts* (Boston: Little, Brown, 1978), 246.
10. Quoted in "Congressional Leaders Predicting Major Revisions to Budget," *Boston Globe*, February 4, 1985, 4.
11. Quoted in, respectively, Martin Tolchin, "How to Win Friends and Influence Foreign Policy," *New York Times*, February 19, 1984, E4, and Pear, "Immigration Bill Dies," ibid., A16.
12. Steven R. Weisman, "Reagan Lauds Congress despite Failures," *New York Times*, November 20, 1983, 1, and Martin Tolchin, "If This is Gridlock, Where's the Traffic Cop?," ibid., October 9, 1984, 6.
13. William J. Keefe, *Congress and the American People* (Englewood Cliffs, N.J.: Prentice-Hall, 1980), 172.
14. Norman J. Ornstein, "The House and the Senate in a New Congress," in *The New Congress*, ed. Thomas E. Mann and Norman J. Ornstein (Washington, D.C.: American Enterprise Institute, 1981), 382.
15. Peter Laslett has written of legislators: "They are quite well aware that however intense the public feeling may be on certain issues and however well organized and powerful may be the pressure behind certain attitudes, consensus of the type they can expect to discover within their own group cannot exist over the whole society." "The Face to Face Society," in *Philosophy, Politics, and Society*, ed. Peter Laslett (Oxford: Blackwell, 1956), 170.
16. Quoted in Pamela Fessler, "The Fiscal 1986 Reagan Budget: The Realities of Deficit-Cutting," *Congressional Quarterly Weekly Report*, February 9, 1985, 215.
17. James Madison, "The Federalist No. 52," in Alexander Hamilton, John Jay, and James Madison, *The Federalist* (1788; reprint, New York: Modern Library, n.d.), 343.
18. Jane J. Mansbridge, *Beyond Adversary Democracy* (Chicago: University of Chicago Press, 1983), 288.
19. The analysis in Jurgen Habermas, *Legitimation Crisis* (Boston: Beacon, 1975), serves as the basis for most discussions of a crisis of legitimacy and the need for continual legitimation of the political system in capitalist societies. For applications of the concept to congressional behavior, see Philip Brenner,

The Limits and Possibilities of Congress (New York: St. Martin's, 1983), 121-129, and Lawrence C. Dodd, "Congress, the Constitution, and the Crisis of Legitimation," in *Congress Reconsidered*, 2nd ed., ed. Lawrence C. Dodd and Bruce I. Oppenheimer (Washington, D.C.: CQ Press, 1981), 411-418.

20. Choper has warned that a string of antimajoritarian rulings by the Supreme Court could "animate a public sentiment that it has but a gossamer claim to legitimacy in a democratic society." On the other hand, he acknowledges that if the Supreme Court justices "were totally to abandon their role as educators and supervisors of the national conscience they would be regarded with disdain as much as or more than if they were to seek to impose their personal views and so revise all legislative and executive policies." Jesse H. Choper, *Judicial Review and the National Political Process* (Chicago: University of Chicago Press, 1980), 139 and 162. The role of the Supreme Court and judicial review in a system of representative democracy is also a chief concern in John Hart Ely, *Democracy and Distrust* (Cambridge: Harvard University Press, 1980).

21. Alan Wolfe, "Presidential Power and the Crisis of Modernization," in *Rethinking the Presidency*, ed. Thomas E. Cronin (Boston: Little, Brown, 1982), 139-152.

22. Anthony King, "How to Strengthen Legislatures—Assuming That We Want To," in *The Role of the Legislature in Western Democracies*, ed. Norman J. Ornstein (Washington, D.C.: American Enterprise Institute, 1981), 84.

23. Quoted in "What's Wrong with Congress—As Insiders See It," *U.S. News & World Report*, December 3, 1984, 39.

24. Quoted in Steven V. Roberts, "A Movement to Do Something about Filibusters," *New York Times*, February 11, 1983, 16.

25. David R. Mayhew, *Congress: The Electoral Connection* (New Haven: Yale University Press, 1974), 141 and 145.

26. Remarks in "Discussion: The Role of the Legislature in a Presidential System," in Ornstein, *Role of the Legislature*, 69.

27. Cass R. Sunstein, "Public Values, Private Interests, and the Equal Protection Clause," 1982 *Supreme Court Review*, 144.

28. Wilson Carey McWilliams, "Democracy and the Citizen: Community, Dignity, and the Crisis of Contemporary Politics in America," in *How Democratic Is the Constitution?*, ed. Robert A. Goldwin and William A. Schambra (Washington, D.C.: American Enterprise Institute, 1981), 92-93.

Index

Abramowitz, Alan I. - 36n
"Accommodating" budgets - 150
Adversary democracy - 3, 4, 18-19, 159-160
  consensus and - 129
  information for - 113-115
  representation and - 23-24
Agenda setting - 108-110
Agriculture Committee, House - 62-65
Agriculture Committee, Senate - 65
Appropriations Committee, House - 68-72, 149-150
Appropriations Committee, Senate - 72, 149-150
Aranson, Peter - 157n
Armed Services Committee, House - 62, 63, 65
Arms Control Export Act of 1976 - 124
Arnold, R. Douglas - 49, 58n, 95, 99n

Backdoor spending - 149
Baker, Howard H., Jr. - 161
Balutis, Alan P. - 119n
Barry, Brian - 157n
Bauer, Raymond A. - 57n
Bessette, Joseph M. - 50, 52-53, 58n, 59n
Betts, Richard K. - 128, 132, 143n
Bibby, John F. - 21n, 121n

Black, Charles L. Jr. - 56n
Bond, Jon R. - 57n
Brenner, Philip - 48, 55, 56, 58n, 59n, 127, 134, 138-139, 142n, 144n, 167n-168n
Broomfield, William S. - 126, 142n
Browning, Edgar K. - 157n
Browning, Jacqueline M. - 157n
Bruff, Harold H. - 59n
Budget Committee, House - 68, 69, 151
Budget and Impoundment Act of 1974 - 148-149
Budgetary process - 53-54
  adversary pressures on - 145-147
  in Congress - 148-151
  net effect of - 155-156
  and options for financing government programs - 147-148
  use of reconciliation in - 151-155, 158n
Burger, Warren E. - 53
Burnham, David - 58n
Byrd, Robert C. - 127, 143n

Campaign financing - 31-35
Capitalism, ideology of - 55
Carter, Jimmy - 140
Cater, Douglass - 98n
Cavanagh, Thomas E. - 58n
Chace, James - 128, 130, 132, 143n

Challengers
  campaign financing and - 31-32
  recognition of, during elections -
  31
Choper, Jesse H. - 168*n*
Clausen, Aage R. - 118*n*
Cloture - 87-88
Cohodas, Nadine - 20*n*, 21*n*, 59*n*,
  167*n*
Commission on Administrative Review, House - 85, 116
Committee bill - 110
Committee for the Free World - 132
Committee report - 110
Committee of the Whole, House - 82,
  84
Committees. *See* Congressional committees
Common interest - 18
Computer usage in Congress - 47,
  105-106
Congress
  budget process in - 148-151
  as democratic body - 1, 17-19
  evaluating - 161-164
  foreign policy and role of - 123-
  126, 133-144
  ideology as source of conflict between president and - 54-55
  impact of computers on - 47
  information resources of - 103-106
  legitimacy of - 165-166
  organizational structure of - 44-46
  the president and - 39-56
  procedures in - 81-91
Congress, members of
  information available to - 46-47
  reelection concerns of - 48-49
  as representatives of local interests
  - 39. *See also* Congressional representation
Congressional Black Caucus - 96
Congressional budget - 53
Congressional Budget Act of 1974 -
  53-54
Congressional Budget Office - 53, 104
Congressional committees - 61-76.
  See also House committees; Senate
  committees

constituency-oriented - 62-66, 73,
  75, 76*n*-77*n*
  policy-oriented - 66-68, 73
  prestige - 68-71
  Senate - 71-73
  sources of adversary and unitary
  modes in - 73-75
  voting cues and - 85
Congressional constituencies; variations in - 42-44
Congressional decision making,
  types of information relevant to -
  106-108
Congressional elections - 50-52. *See
  also* House campaigns; Senatorial
  campaigns
  ability of president to affect - 50-51
  financing of - 31-35
  party presentation of issue conflicts during - 30
  voter ignorance and - 31. *See also*
  Voter ignorance
Congressional hearing - 110
Congressional parochialism - 48-49
Congressional representation - 39
  conflicts regarding presidential
  and - 41-48
Congressional Research Service - 104
Congressional staff, size of - 46, 103-
  104
Congressional Steel Caucus - 96
Consensus, foreign policy and - 127-
  133
Constituency committees - 62-66, 73,
  75, 76*n*-77*n*
  U.S. policy committees - 66-67
Constituencies. *See* Congressional
  constituencies
Constituents, gaining trust of - 27
Conte, Silvio O. - 164
Cooper, Ann - 99*n*
Cooper, Joseph - 120*n*
Corwin, Edwin S. - 56*n*
Crabb, Cecil V., Jr. - 125-126, 132,
  137, 140, 142*n*, 143*n*, 144*n*
Cranston, Alan - 16
Crewdson, John - 14-15, 21*n*
Cronin, Thomas E. - 56*n*, 57*n*, 59*n*,
  142*n*, 168*n*

Crotty, William - 98*n*
Cue network - 45, 84-86, 89, 91, 113, 116
   element of trust in - 117-118
Cummings, Milton C. - 97*n*

Davidson, Roger H. - 20*n*, 48, 56*n*, 58*n*, 97*n*, 98*n*, 99*n*, 119*n*
Davis, Joseph A. - 20*n*
Debate. *See* Floor debate
Deering, Christopher - 61, 63, 76*n*, 77*n*, 78*n*, 79*n*, 99*n*
Deficit financing - 147-148
Deliberation - 90-91
Deliberative institution - 50
Democracy, adversary vs. unitary - 2-4
Democratic Caucus, House - 93
Democratic legitimacy - 164-166
Democratic party
   campaign contributions to - 35
   supporters of - 92
Democratic Study Group - 85, 90, 96
Destler, I. M. - 127, 128, 134-137, 142*n*, 143*n*, 144*n*
Dexter, Lewis Anthony - 56*n*, 57*n*
Discrimination, anti-Hispanic - 15
District interests, voting on matters of - 2-3
Diversity - competitiveness hypothesis - 43, 57*n*
Division vote - 83
Dodd, Lawrence C. - 76*n*, 99*n*, 142*n*, 168*n*
Dole, Robert - 34, 162
Downey, Thomas J. - 33
Drew, Elizabeth - 37*n*
Dumanoski, Dianne - 121*n*

Eckhardt, Bob - 42, 56*n*
Eckhart, Dennis E. - 2, 3
Economic policy, and congressional budget process - 145-156
Edwards, George C., III - 44-46, 57*n*, 59*n*
Elections. *See* Congressional elections; House campaigns; Senatorial campaigns
Ellwood, John W. - 157*n*
Ely, John Hart - 168*n*

Energy and Commerce Committee, House - 32, 66
Environmental issues - 2
Environmental Study Conference - 96
Equal representation - 17
Equality, immigration reform and - 15-16
Executive branch
   organizational structure of - 44-46
   size of staff of - 46
Executive budget - 53

Family unity, immigration reform and - 15
Federal Reserve Board - 146, 156
Felton, John - 142*n*, 143*n*, 144*n*
Fenno, Richard F., Jr. - 27-29, 36*n*, 43, 56*n*, 57*n*, 58*n*, 59*n*, 76*n*, 78*n*, 79*n*, 98*n*, 109-110, 118, 120*n*, 162, 167*n*
Fessler, Pamela - 167*n*
Filibusters - 87, 88
Finance Committee, Senate - 72
Finifter, Ada W. - 143*n*
Fiorina, Morris P. - 57*n*, 58*n*
Fiscal policy - 156
Fisher, Joseph - 98*n*
Fisher, Louis - 59*n*, 157*n*
Floor debate - 88-90
Floor procedures - 87-89
Foreign Affairs Committee, House - 78*n*
Foreign Assistance Act of 1976 - 133
Foreign policy
   changing congressional role in - 136-141
   Congress, the presidency and - 123-126
   consensus and - 127-133
   democracy and - 128-129, 137
   formulation and implementation of - 133-136
Formulation stage of policy-making process - 110-112
Fox, Harrison W., Jr. - 121*n*
Franck, Thomas M. - 136-137, 140, 141, 144*n*
Frank, Barney - 2
Franklin, Grace A. - 109, 120*n*, 157*n*

Frantzich, Stephen E. - 57*n*, 58*n*, 105-
108, 115, 119*n*, 120*n*, 121*n*
Freeman, J. Lieper - 98*n*

Garza, Francisco - 8
Gelb, Leslie H. - 128, 132, 143*n*
Gellhorn, Ernest - 59*n*
George, Alexander - 57*n*, 128-130,
132-133, 143*n*
Gerston, Larry N. - 143*n*
Goldenberg, Edie N. - 36*n*
Goldwater, Barry - 126, 142*n*
Goldwin, Robert A. - 168*n*
Goodman, Walter - 143*n*
Gramm, Phil - 92
Granat, Diane - 142*n*
Greenstein, Fred I. - 54, 59*n*
Greenstone, J. David - 57*n*
Griffith, Ernest S. - 98*n*
"Guest worker" programs - 8-9, 16
Gurwitt, Rob - 167*n*

Habermas, Jurgen - 167*n*
Hale, Dennis - 58*n*, 59*n*, 120*n*
Hamilton, Alexander - 167*n*
Hamilton, Lee H. - 126, 127, 133-134,
142*n*, 143*n*, 162-163
Hammond, Susan Webb - 121*n*
Harris, Lou - 161
Havemann, Joel - 157*n*
Heaphey, James J. - 119*n*
Heclo, Hugo - 57*n*, 59*n*, 98*n*
Hesburgh, Theodore - 15
Hinckley, Barbara - 35*n*, 36*n*, 59*n*
Hispanic interests, immigration re-
form bill and - 5, 6, 8, 10, 15
Hodgson, Godfrey - 144*n*
Hollings, Ernest F. - 88
Holt, Pat M. - 125-126, 132, 137, 140,
142*n*, 143*n*, 144*n*
House campaigns, incumbent-chal-
lenger recognition during - 31
House Commission on Adminis-
trative Review - 85, 116
House committees, classification of -
61-62
House Information Systems - 47
House of Representatives - 97
committees of - 61-62. *See also*
House Committees

Huddleston, Walter D. - 7, 11, 15
Human rights, foreign policy and -
140-141
Huntington, Samuel P. - 55, 59*n*
Hyde, Henry J. - 5, 163

Ideology, as source of conflict between president and Congress - 54-
55
Immigration and Nationality Act,
1965 amendments to - 15
*Immigration and Naturalization Service
v. Chadha* - 53, 59*n*
Immigration reform - 5-17. *See also*
Immigration Reform and Control
Act
Immigration Reform and Control Act
of 1983
common interest regarding - 10-17
conflicting interests regarding - 7-
10
congressional action on - 5-7
Incumbents
campaign financing and - 31-32
electoral advantage of - 50-51
recognition of, during election - 31
voter ignorance and - 25, 26
Information resources of Congress -
103-106
types of - 106-108
versus information resources of executive branch - 46-47
Interest representation - 40-49
Interests - 17-18
Interior Committee, House - 62, 63
International Security Assistance Act
of 1978 - 133
"Iron triangles" - 91, 98*n*
"Issue networks" - 98*n*

Jacobson, Gary C. - 35*n*, 36*n*, 37*n*, 51,
59*n*, 98*n*
Jay, John - 167*n*
Jefferson, Thomas - 40, 56*n*
Jones, Charles O. - 35*n*, 37*n*, 56*n*, 58*n*,
98*n*, 120*n*, 134, 143*n*

Kahn, Ronald C. - 57*n*
Keefe, William J. - 99*n*, 167*n*
Kennan, George - 131
Kennedy, Edward M. - 16

Kennedy, John F. - 40, 56n, 124
Kernell, Samuel - 59n
Key, V. O. - 58n
King, Anthony - 56n, 98n, 106, 119n, 120n, 165, 168n
Kingdon, John W. - 118n, 119n, 120n, 121n
Kirkland, Lane - 8-9
Kohlmeier, Louis M., Jr. - 19n
Kovenock, David - 119n
Kozak, David C. - 58n, 119n
Krasner, Stephen D. - 125, 142n

Labor unions, and immigration reform bill - 8-9
Ladd, Everett C. - 98n
Laslett, Peter - 35n-36n, 167n
Leach, Jim - 33, 34
League of Conservation Voters - 2
League of United Latin American Citizens - 10
Legislative cue taking - 45. *See also* Cue network
Legislative Reference Service - 104
Legislative Reorganization Act of 1946 - 104
Legislative veto - 52-53
Legitimacy, concept of - 164-166
Legitimation stage of policy-making process - 112-113
Lewis, Anthony - 127, 143n
Lewis, Wilfred - 158n
Light, Paul - 110, 120
Lineberry, Robert L. - 143n
Logrolling - 63
Loomis, Burdett A. - 99n
Lowi, Theodore - 79n, 157n
Lungren, Dan - 20n

Maass, Arthur - 36n, 44, 57n, 78n, 79n
Macartney, John D. - 58n, 119n
McConnell, Grant - 42, 43, 56n, 57n
McFarlane, Robert C. - 125
MacKenzie, G. Calvin - 120n
Macmahon, Arthur W. - 106, 119n
McWilliams, Wilson Carey - 168n
Madison, James - 1, 19, 166, 167n
Maisel, Louis - 120n
Majority rule - 3, 17, 20n

Malbin, Michael J. - 16, 21n, 105, 111-114, 119n, 120n, 121n
Manley, John F. - 78n
Mann, Thomas E. - 36n, 51, 58n, 99n, 120n, 144n, 157n, 167n
Mansbridge, Jane J. - 3, 18-19, 20n, 22n, 36n, 77n, 78n, 79n, 101-103, 115, 117, 118n, 119n, 121n, 129, 143n, 167n
Mathias, Charles McC. - 47, 165, 166
Mathis, Dawson - 64n
Matthews, Donald R. - 57n, 98n, 116, 118n, 120n, 121n
Mavroules, Nicholas - 2
Mayhew, David R. - 19n-20n, 26, 35n, 58n, 78n, 166, 168n
Mazzoli, Romano L. - 6, 7, 11, 13-15
Mexican-American Legal Defense and Education Fund - 10
Meyer, Laurence - 157n
Mondale, Walter - 47
Monetary policy - 156
Morrison, Bruce A. - 59n
Moynihan, Daniel Patrick - 46
MX missile production - 2
Myers, Michael - 56n

National Association of Counties - 7
National Council of La Raza - 8, 10
National interest
  concept of - 12, 130
  voting on matters of - 2-3
National League of Cities - 7
Nelson, Michael - 48-49, 56n, 58n
Neustadt, Richard E. - 45, 109, 120n
Nixon, Richard - 124, 132, 142n
Noll, Roger - 157n
Nordlinger, Eric A. - 21n-22n, 59n
Northeast-Midwest Congressional Coalition - 96
Nuclear Nonproliferation Act of 1978 - 124

O'Brien, Lawrence - 54, 59n
Ochoa, Maria - 167n
Office of Technology Assessment (OTA) - 104, 115
Oleszek, Walter - 20n, 56n, 97n, 98n
Olson, Mancur, Jr. - 36n

O'Neill, Thomas P., Jr. - 5-7, 54, 125, 135
Oppenheimer, Bruce I. - 76, 99*n*, 142*n*, 168*n*
Ornstein, Norman J. - 36*n*, 58*n*, 79*n*, 97*n*, 98*n*, 99*n*, 119*n*, 120*n*, 144*n*, 157*n*, 167*n*, 168*n*
Ottinger, Richard L. - 165

PACs. *See* Political action committees
Parker, Glenn R. - 77*n*, 78*n*
Parker, Suzanne L. - 77*n*, 78*n*
Parties. *See* Political parties
Party caucuses - 93
Peabody, Robert L. - 97*n*, 98*n*, 99*n*
Pear, Robert - 20*n*, 167*n*
Penner, Rudolph G. - 59*n*
Pitkin, Hanna Fenichel - 50, 55, 58*n*, 59*n*
Plattner, Andy - 78*n*
Policy committees - 66-68, 73
  versus constituency committees - 66-67
Policy consensus - 130-132
Policy formulation stage - 110-112
Policy-making process
  agenda setting - 108-110
  formulation - 110-112
  legitimation - 112-113
Political action committees (PACs)
  contributions to congressional campaigns by - 33-34
  contributions to congressional committees by - 78*n*
Political information - 106, 107, 109
Political parties
  role of - 91-97
  voter ignorance and - 30-31
Politics of inclusion - 95
Polsby, Nelson W. - 97*n*
Pool, Ithiel de Sola - 57*n*
Porter, H. Owen - 106, 119*n*-120*n*, 121*n*
Presidency, legitimacy of - 165
President
  ability of to affect outcome of congressional elections - 50-51
  failures and successes attributed to - 25-26
  foreign policy and - 123-126

ideology as source of conflict between Congress and - 54-55
  as representative of national interests - 39,41. *See also* Presidential representation
Presidential campaigns, party presentation of issue conflicts during - 30
Presidential representation - 39
  conflicts regarding congressional and - 41-48
Presidential veto - 52
Prestige committees - 68-71, 73
Price, David - 76*n*, 79*n*, 120*n*
Procedural consensus - 132-133
Proportional outcomes - 3, 20*n*
Proportional representation (PR) - 44
Public interest, concept of - 11-12
Public Works and Transportation Committee, House - 62, 63, 65

Ragsdale, Lyn - 59*n*
Ray, Bruce A. - 77*n*, 78*n*
Reagan, Ronald - 5, 124-125, 128, 131, 135, 143*n*, 152, 162
Representational process - 23-35
Republican party, supporters of - 92
Republican Study Committee - 85, 90
Richardson, James D. - 56*n*
Rieselbach, Leroy N. - 77*n*, 157*n*
Riker, William H. - 143*n*
Ripley, Randall B. - 109, 120*n*, 157*n*
Roberts, Steven V. - 20*n*, 59*n*, 167*n*, 168*n*
Robinson, Michael J. - 36*n*
Rodino, Peter W., Jr. - 13, 20*n*
Rogers, David - 143*n*
Rohde, David - 58*n*, 98*n*, 119*n*
Roybal, Edward R. - 5
Rules Committee, House - 69, 81-82, 86

Salamon, Lester M. - 57*n*
Schambra, William A. - 168*n*
Schattschneider, E. E. - 36*n*, 94, 98*n*, 99*n*
Schick, Allen - 59*n*, 157*n*, 158*n*
Schneider, Jerrold E. - 99*n*, 138, 144*n*
Schneier, Edward V., Jr. - 99*n*, 119*n*, 120*n*

Schumer, Charles E. - 167n
Science and Technology Committee, House - 63
Select Commission on Immigration and Refugee Policy - 5
Select Committee on Committees - 74
Senate
 decision-making process in - 86-87
 structure of - 97
 unanimous consent agreements in - 86-88
 use of cloture in - 87-88
Senate committees - 71-73
Senate Computer Center - 47
Senatorial campaigns, incumbent-challenger recognition during - 31
Sensenbrenner, F. James, Jr. - 20n
Shabecoff, Philip - 20n
Shannon, James M. - 33
Shepsle, Kenneth - 77n
Simpson, Alan K. - 5, 7-10, 12-16, 21n, 54
Sinclair, Barbara - 99n
Small Business Committee, House - 65
Smith, Steven S. - 61, 63, 76n, 77n, 78n, 79n, 99n
Smith, William French - 5, 7-8
Spanier, John - 137, 144n
Speakes, Larry - 135
Stein, Charles - 20n
Stennis, John C. - 161
Stern, Paula - 138, 144n
Stevenson, Adlai, III - 126, 142n
Stimson, James A. - 57n, 98n, 116, 118n, 120n, 121n
Stockman, David A. - 64
Subcommittee Bill of Rights - 68
Subcommittees, organization of - 62, 73-74
"Subgovernments" - 91
Sundquist, James L. - 56n, 58n, 119n, 127, 132, 134, 138, 140, 142n, 143n, 144n
"Sunshine" rule - 75
Sunstein, Cass R. - 168n
Swift, Al - 119n

Targeted mail - 36n
Technical information - 106-110

Teller vote - 83
Thomas, Norman C. - 56n
Thurber, James A. - 157n
Tolchin, Martin - 120n, 142n, 167n
Traugott, Michael W. - 36n
Trollope, Anthony - 120n
Turner, Julius - 99n

Unanimous consent agreements, Senate - 86
Unekis, Joseph K. - 77n
Unitary democracy - 3-4, 17-19, 159-160
 consensus and - 129
 information for - 115-118
 presidential representation and - 39
 representation and - 23-24
U.S. Chamber of Commerce, and immigration reform bill - 9
Uslaner, Eric M. - 137, 144n

Value consensus - 129-130
Vanik, Charles A. - 120n
Veterans Affairs Committee, House - 65
Vetos - 52-53
"Vital interests" - 143n
Vogler, David J. - 76n, 99n, 157n
Voice vote - 83
Voter ignorance
 congressional democracy and - 28-30
 consequences of - 25-27
 methods in which congressional members contribute to - 27-28
 parties and - 30-31
Voter knowledge - 24-25
Votes, recording of - 82-84
Voting cues - 45, 84-86, 89, 91, 113

Waldman, Sidney - 99n
Waltz, Kenneth N. - 137-139, 144n
War Powers Resolution of 1973 - 124, 133, 135, 141
Watson, Richard A. - 56n
Ways and Means Committee, House - 32, 68-70, 72
Weber, Max - 102

Wehr, Elizabeth - 77*n*
Weinstein, Michael - 157*n*
Weisband, Edward - 136-137, 140, 141, 144*n*
Weisman, Steven R. - 142*n*, 167*n*
White, Byron R. - 53

White, Theodore H. - 142*n*
Whittle, Richard - 143*n*
Wilson, Woodrow - 40, 56*n*
Wolfe, Alan - 55, 59*n*, 168*n*
Wolfinger, Raymond E. - 99*n*
Wright, Jim - 125, 161

DATE DUE

APR 04 '94
FEB 18 '95
JAN 31 '96
FEB 1 3 1997
MAR 3 1 1997
FEB 28 '98

261-2500

Printed
in USA